Reading

FORWARD

BASIC 2

BASIC 2

Series Editors Bin-na Yang, Dong-sook Kim

Project Editors Jung-ah Lee, Mina Song, Mi-youn Woo, Jee-young Song, Kyung-hee Kim, Na-hyun Ahn, Eun-kyung Kim

Contributing Writers Patrick Ferraro, Henry John Amen IV, John Boswell, Robert Vernon, Keeran Murphy, Peter Morton

Illustrators Seol-hee Kim, Hyun-il Bang, Hyun-jin Choi, Hyo-sil Lee

Design Ho-hyun Bang, Hyun-jung Jang, Yeon-joo Kim

Editorial Designer In-sun Lee

Sales Ki-young Han, Kyung-koo Lee, In-gyu Park, Cheol-gyo Jeong, Nam-jun Kim, Woo-hyun Lee

Marketers Hye-sun Park, Kyung-jin Nam, Ji-won Lee, Yeo-jin Kim

Copyright © 2015 by NE Neungyule, Inc.

First Printing 15 June 2015

11th Printing 15 September 2023

ISBN 979-11-253-0797-6 53740

INTRODUCTION

★
★
★

Reading Forward is a six-level series of three progressive steps: Basic, Intermediate, and Advanced. Based on the essential needs of young students, the series focuses on a specific goal: expanding vocabulary and knowledge. This goal guides all of the content and activities in the series. The first step of the series will enlarge vocabulary, and the later steps will increase knowledge. Thus, the series will eventually help students improve their reading comprehension.

Each book of Reading Forward is composed of 20 units. The number of words used in each reading passage is as follows.

Step 3
Reading Forward
Advanced
for Knowledge
1 : 240 – 260 words
2 : 260 – 280 words

Step 2
Reading Forward
Intermediate
for Vocabulary & Knowledge
1 : 200 – 220 words
2 : 220 – 240 words

Step 1
Reading Forward
Basic
for Vocabulary
1 : 150 – 170 words
2 : 170 – 190 words

Key Features of Reading Forward Series

– Current, high-interest topics are developed in an easy way so that students can understand them. These subjects can hold their attention and keep them motivated to read forward.

– Comprehension checkup questions presented in the series are based on standardized test questions. These can help students prepare for English tests at school, as well as official English language tests.

– Each unit is designed to enlarge vocabulary by presenting intensive activities for learning vocabulary at both the beginning and the end of each unit. Students can learn the key words in each passage and effectively improve their vocabulary.

FORMAT

Vocabulary Preview
Before reading each passage, students can preview the key words through two activities: definition – word matching and finding synonyms or antonyms.

Before Reading
The question before each passage allows students to think about the topic by relating it to their lives. It also helps students become interested in the passage before reading it.

Reading
This part serves as the main passage of the unit, and it explains an intriguing and instructive topic in great depth. As students progress through the book, the content of these passages becomes more and more substantial.

Reading Comprehension
The reading is followed by different types of questions, which test understanding of the passage. The various types of questions focus on important reading skills, such as understanding the main idea and organization of the passage, identifying details, and drawing inferences.

Strategic Summary / Organizer

Each unit includes a strategic summary or organizer of the main reading passage. It gives students a better understanding of the important points and organization of the passage. These exercises focus on further development of effective reading comprehension skills.

Vocabulary Review

A review of the key vocabulary concludes each unit. Three types of exercises test understanding of new words: matching definitions, identifying synonyms and antonyms, and completing sentences with the correct words in context.

Word Book

A list of the key words from each unit is presented in a handy book for convenience. It provides students with an easy reference to new vocabulary.

MP3 Files

Audio recordings of all reading passages are available to be downloaded for free at www.nebooks.co.kr.

TABLE OF CONTENTS

Unit 01   JOBS   An Interview with a Game Tester · 9

Unit 02   CULTURE   Jazz Funerals · 13

Unit 03   TEENS   Terry's Problem · 17

Unit 04   ANIMALS   The Pet Blood Bank · 21

Unit 05   PLACES   The Salar de Uyuni · 25

Unit 06   LITERATURE   A Sherlock Holmes Story · 29

Unit 07   SPORTS   Ball Possession in Soccer · 33

Unit 08   PEOPLE   Stevie Wonder · 37

Unit 09   FOOD   Tomatoes · 41

Unit 10   ECONOMY   Undercover Marketing · 45

Reading Forward

Unit 11	FESTIVALS	Songkran · 49
Unit 12	PSYCHOLOGY	Why People Overeat · 53
Unit 13	SCIENCE	Satellites · 57
Unit 14	SOCIETY	Pro Bono · 61
Unit 15	ENTERTAINMENT	Billy Elliot the Musical · 65
Unit 16	HUMAN BODY	Runner's High · 69
Unit 17	EDUCATION	The Pygmalion Effect · 73
Unit 18	TRAVEL	Asahiyama Zoo · 77
Unit 19	FASHION	The History of Wigs · 81
Unit 20	ISSUES	Animal Testing · 85

Unit ★ 01

JOBS

A Connect each word to its correct definition.

1 to need something • • *a.* test

2 to issue a new product for sale • • *b.* require

3 to use something to see if it works well • • *c.* release

4 the ability to wait without becoming annoyed • • *d.* patience

B Write the word that has the opposite meaning of each word.

cause various problem fix

1 same : _____ 2 result : _____

3 break : _____ 4 solution : _____

★ An Interview with a Game Tester

This is an interview with Robert Watson. He is a game tester for a famous computer game company in Los Angeles.

Q: What does a game tester do?

A: Just like companies test their new products before selling them, we test new games to see if they work properly. (①) We closely check each game by playing it in many different ways. (②) And we also help them figure out the cause. (③) When all the problems are fixed, the company can release the game.

10   (④) Even afterwards, we need to correct other errors found by users.

Q: _____(A)_____

A: My brother is a game designer. I like to play various kinds of games, so he often asked me to check the games he made. Because he saw my talent for computer games, he suggested that I become a game tester. Besides, it was

15   exciting to be the first person to try out new games. So I decided to become a game tester!

Q: What skills do game testers need?

A: Basically, game testers need knowledge about computer systems. Plus, they should be good communicators

20   to explain problems clearly to game designers. Most importantly, patience is required because they test the same game again and again.

READING COMPREHENSION

1 What is the interview mainly about?

    a. How to test new products
    b. Testing new games as a job
    c. Working as a game programmer
    d. What makes a new game successful

2 Why does Robert mention the underlined sentence?

    a. To explain how difficult game testing is

    b. To compare game testers with salesmen

    c. To contrast game testing with product testing

    d. To give a general idea of what game testers do

3 Where would the following sentence best fit?

> If we discover any bugs or mistakes, we report them to the game programmers and designers.

    a. ①   *b.* ②   *c.* ③   *d.* ④

4 What is the best choice for blank (A)?

    a. Why did you choose this job?   *b.* Who do you usually work with?

    c. What is difficult about your job?   *d.* What do you like about your job?

5 Why did Robert's brother recommend that Robert should become a game tester?

_____

6 What is NOT needed to be a game tester?

    a. A technical understanding of computers

    b. Communication skills to clearly define problems

    c. The ability to do one thing over and over

    d. The ability to sell products to people

STRATEGIC SUMMARY

Fill in the blanks with the correct words.

In an interview, Robert Watson talks about his job as a game tester. He explains that game testers make sure that there are no _____ in new games. He became _____ in game testing because of his brother, who is a game designer. Finally, he explains what _____ game testers must have. They need knowledge about computers, good communication skills, and lots of _____.

> skills   company   problems   patience   interested

VOCABULARY REVIEW

A Complete the sentences with the words in the box. (Change the form if needed.)

try out	decide	talent	report	discover

1 She showed a _____ for singing at an early age.

2 They have _____ the results of a survey to the doctor.

3 Let's _____ the old machine to check if it is still working.

4 He _____ to forget the past so that he could make a fresh start.

B Find the word that has a similar meaning to the underlined word.

1 Please watch closely. This is an important part of the movie.

    a. generally   *b.* often   *c.* always   *d.* carefully

2 No matter how hard I tried, I couldn't figure out how to open the box.

    a. help out   *b.* check out   *c.* find out   *d.* hand out

C Choose the best word to complete each sentence.

1 Julia couldn't understand the situation, so I _____ it to her.

    a. explained   *b.* gave   *c.* handed   *d.* compared

2 I joined a writing club to improve my writing _____.

    a. gifts   *b.* skills   *c.* tutors   *d.* masters

3 He _____ we should have dinner first and then watch a movie.

    a. played   *b.* checked   *c.* complained   *d.* suggested

4 If there are any grammatical errors in this writing, can you _____ them?

    a. ruin   *b.* create   *c.* correct   *d.* exchange

Unit ★ 02

CULTURE

A Connect each word to its correct definition.

1 to cry out in sadness • • **a.** wail

2 an area where dead people are buried • • **b.** slave

3 a group of people who play music together • • **c.** band

4 a person who is forced to work for his or her owner • • **d.** cemetery

B Write the word that has the opposite meaning of each word.

cheerful	dress	wild	dead

1 calm : _____   **2** alive : _____

3 gloomy : _____   **4** take off : _____

Normally, funerals are sad and serious. People dressed in black often cry and wail. However, African Americans in New Orleans developed a different tradition. They sometimes have "jazz funerals."

Jazz funerals _____(A)_____ at first. As a car takes the
5 body to the cemetery, family and friends of the dead follow quietly. (①) A brass band also marches with them, playing sad music. (②) The band starts playing cheerful music, and the beat gets faster and wilder. (③) People on the street often join the march to sing and dance to the music. (④)

The origin of jazz funerals goes back to the 18th century, a period

when there was still slavery. The slaves lived hard lives and thought death could release them from slavery. So they celebrated the freedom of the dead by singing and dancing. They also thought singing and dancing helped the dead find their way to heaven. In the 20th century, people started to play jazz at funerals. These funerals became known as "jazz funerals."

Although people at jazz funerals have fun, they still show love for the dead like people do at all other funerals.

READING
COMPREHENSION

1 **What is the best title for the passage?**

   a. The History of Slaves in America
   b. The Popularity of Jazz in New Orleans
   c. A Unique Funeral Tradition in New Orleans
   d. Differences between American and African Culture

2 What is the best choice for blank (A)?

    a. are held in a church   *b.* seem like usual funerals

    c. include traditional music   *d.* are different from other funerals

3 Where would the following sentence best fit?

> However, everything changes when they return from the cemetery.

    a. ①   *b.* ②   *c.* ③   *d.* ④

4 What is the 3rd paragraph mainly about?

    a. Why Africans became slaves

    b. How jazz funerals originated

    c. When slavery ended in America

    d. Why Africans consider funerals important

5 Why did slaves in America celebrate death by singing and dancing?

_____

6 What is NOT mentioned about jazz funerals?

    a. Which area of America they are held in

    b. Who can join them

    c. Why they are popular in America

    d. What kind of music is played there

STRATEGIC ORGANIZER

Fill in the blanks with the correct words.

Jazz Funerals in New Orleans

What they are like
- They begin like other _____ funerals.
- Later, the brass band plays _____ music, and people sing and dance.

How funerals became an event to celebrate
- African slaves thought death could make them _____.
- They thought the dead could find a way to _____.

| free | joyful | normal | heaven | tradition |

★ ★ ★
VOCABULARY REVIEW

A Complete the sentences with the words in the box. (Change the form if needed.)

usual	serious	march	funeral	freedom

1 The children started to _____ down the street.

2 His grandfather died, and the _____ was held the next day.

3 We need to have a _____ talk about this upsetting problem.

4 Steve woke up later than _____, so he couldn't eat breakfast.

B Find the word that has a similar meaning to the underlined word.

1 I normally stay at home on weekends.

   a. possibly   *b.* seldom   *c.* usually   *d.* never

2 People on the stage danced to the beat of a fast song.

   a. step   *b.* noise   *c.* speed   *d.* rhythm

C Choose the best word to complete each sentence.

1 Eating turkey on Thanksgiving Day is a(n) _____ in America.

   a. symbol   *b.* process   *c.* advance   *d.* tradition

2 Sue is going to _____ from her trip to Europe next weekend.

   a. return   *b.* receive   *c.* display   *d.* produce

3 The _____ of this custom remains unknown.

   a. tool   *b.* origin   *c.* material   *d.* substance

4 The movie is set in Rome during a(n) _____ of conflict.

   a. slave   *b.* person   *c.* period   *d.* influence

TEENS

VOCABULARY PREVIEW

A Connect each word to its correct definition.

1 usual or natural •   • *a.* fear

2 a formal talk given to many people •   • *b.* shake

3 to move up and down or side to side quickly •   • *c.* speech

4 a feeling of being afraid of someone or something •   • *d.* normal

B Write the word that has the opposite meaning of each word.

bright accept public interested

1 deny : _____   *2* dark : _____

3 bored : _____   *4* private : _____

★ *Terry's Problem*

Dear Dr. Page,

I have to give a speech in front of my whole class next week. I feel so nervous about it. Every time I speak in public, my hands shake, 5 my face turns bright red, and my heart beats rapidly. What can I do?

Terry

Dear Terry,

You may have a fear of public speaking. 10 This is very common because no one wants to make mistakes in front of other people. You can overcome this fear by following these tips.

First, remember that getting nervous is normal. (①) In fact, a little fear can help you! (②) When you become nervous, your body releases a hormone called adrenaline. (③) So try to accept your nervousness and make 15 good use of it. (④)

Next, try not to be afraid of the audience. <u>Consider them as your friends.</u> When you speak, smile and look your audience in the eye. This way, they will become more interested. And that makes giving the speech easier.

Finally, prepare for your speech carefully. Remember that 20 _____(A)_____. Giving the speech to your family or friends can help you! The more familiar you are with the speech, the better your performance will be.

Dr. Page

READING COMPREHENSION

1 What is Dr. Page's advice mainly about?

　　a. Ways to be a good listener

　　b. Advantages of public speaking

　　c. Tips for delivering a funny speech

　　d. How to control a fear of public speaking

2 Why are people afraid of giving a speech in public?

_____

3 Where would the following sentence best fit?

| This makes you lively and gives you more energy to help you perform better. |

a. ①　　　　　　*b.* ②　　　　　　*c.* ③　　　　　　*d.* ④

4 What does the underlined sentence mean?

   a. Treat the audience politely.

   b. Try to learn about the audience.

   c. Think of the audience as people you are familiar with.

   d. Be friendly to the audience to make them your best friends.

5 What is the best choice for blank (A)?

   a. first come, first served   *b.* practice makes perfect

   c. no news is good news   *d.* two heads are better than one

6 If Terry follows the advice, what is he UNLIKELY to do?

   a. Think that fear is a normal thing.

   b. Try not to look into the eyes of the audience.

   c. Prepare for his speech by practicing.

   d. Give the speech to his friends.

STRATEGIC ORGANIZER

Fill in the blanks with the correct words.

The Fear of Public Speaking

Problem
• It comes from not wanting to make _____ in public.

Solutions
• Accept fear as a(n) _____ thing.
• Don't be afraid of the _____ and look them in the eye.
• Prepare a lot and _____ giving the speech to people.

| audience | performance | practice | mistakes | normal |

★ ★ ★
VOCABULARY REVIEW

A Complete the sentences with the words in the box. (Change the form if needed.)

in public	audience	overcome	whole	mistake

1 A single bulb lit up the _____ room brightly.

2 He _____ his injury and finally won the Olympic medal.

3 The _____ clapped and cheered as he ended his speech.

4 He made a fool out of me _____. Everyone laughed at me.

B Find the word that has a similar meaning to the underlined word.

1 When night comes, the temperature drops <u>rapidly</u>.

    a. quickly   *b.* slowly   *c.* normally   *d.* strangely

2 I was very <u>nervous</u> about the final exams.

    a. sad   *b.* calm   *c.* tired   *d.* anxious

C Choose the best word to complete each sentence.

1 I'm _____ with that area because I've visited there many times.

    a. honest   *b.* familiar   *c.* fair   *d.* angry

2 There are many things she must _____ for her wedding.

    a. prepare   *b.* stand   *c.* sign   *d.* test

3 The girl _____ herself to be overweight although she is not.

    a. proves   *b.* considers   *c.* shows   *d.* allows

4 Burning plastic _____ toxic gases into the atmosphere.

    a. invites   *b.* throws   *c.* follows   *d.* releases

Unit ★ 04
ANIMALS

A Connect each word to its correct definition.

1 the state of being alive •   • ***a.*** pet

2 an animal that is kept at home •   • ***b.*** life

3 to give something to help others •   • ***c.*** save

4 to prevent someone from dying or being harmed • • ***d.*** donate

B Write the word that has a similar meaning to each word.

donor	collect	delicious	sick

1 ill : _____   2 tasty : _____

3 giver : _____   4 gather : _____

★ *The Pet Blood Bank*

http://www.petblooduk.org

ABOUT US
PET OWNERS
WHAT WE DO
 COLLECTION
 EDUCATION

FAQs

CONTACT US

Have you heard of Pet Blood Bank in the UK? Like humans, dogs can get hurt and need a blood donation. To help sick dogs across the country, it collects other dogs' blood and gives it to them. Since this program started in 2007, it has saved the lives of thousands of dogs!

5   Many pet owners gladly bring their dogs to have them donate their blood. ① However, not every dog can donate. ② Donor dogs must get a health check first. ③ Dog owners should bring their pets to the doctor at least once a year. ④ Donor dogs have to weigh over 25 kg and be between one and eight years old. They must also have all their *vaccinations up to
10   date. If a donor dog is healthy enough, up to 450 ml of blood will be taken. This amount of blood can save the lives of four other dogs!

Donating blood helps not only sick dogs but also pet owners. The results of the health check can show them important changes in their dog's health. And
15   the donor dogs are given a delicious drink and a biscuit for giving blood!

*vaccination: a shot to prevent a person or animal from getting a disease

READING COMPREHENSION

1 What is the best title for the passage?

  a. Keep Your Dog's Blood Safe
  b. Dogs Helping Humans in Need
  c. Pet Blood Banks vs. Human Blood Banks
  d. Give Your Dog a Chance to Help Other Dogs!

2 What does Pet Blood Bank do to help sick dogs in the UK?

_____

3 Which sentence is NOT needed in the passage?

   a. ①   *b.* ②   *c.* ③   *d.* ④

4 Which dog CANNOT be a donor dog?

   a. Buddy is in good shape.

   b. Molly weighs 20 kilograms.

   c. Max is five years old.

   d. Lucy has all her vaccinations.

5 What is the 3rd paragraph mainly about?

   a. Where the blood is used

   b. How the blood is collected

   c. The process of giving blood

   d. The benefits of blood donation

6 Which is NOT mentioned about Pet Blood Bank?

   a. What kind of work it does

   b. When it started

   c. How it gets blood from dogs

   d. What it gives to donor dogs

STRATEGIC SUMMARY

Fill in the blanks with the correct words.

Pet Blood Bank collects blood from _____ dogs. Then the blood is given to sick dogs to _____ their lives. Before giving blood, dogs must pass a(n) _____ check. They must also be more than 25 kilograms, between one and eight years old, and have all of their vaccinations. By donating blood, donor dogs can also get their health checked and enjoy a(n) _____ snack.

> save   donor   owner   health   delicious

★ ★ ★
VOCABULARY REVIEW

A Complete the sentences with the words in the box. (Change the form if needed.)

health	blood	owner	donation	enough

1 Alice cut her finger, and _____ came out.

2 Mike secretly made a(n) _____ to a charity.

3 This apartment isn't big _____ for a large family.

4 The _____ of this building is the richest man in China.

B Find the word that has the opposite meaning of the underlined word.

1 Make sure all your records are kept up to date.

    a. recent   *b.* modern   *c.* helpful   *d.* out of date

2 Mr. Green gladly accepted my proposal.

    a. slowly   *b.* honestly   *c.* carefully   *d.* unwillingly

C Choose the best word to complete each sentence.

1 This company made a laptop that _____ less than 1 kg.

    a. weighs   *b.* sounds   *c.* compares   *d.* describes

2 Many people thought the _____ of the soccer game was disappointing.

    a. decrease   *b.* result   *c.* matter   *d.* increase

3 Sue was in a serious car accident but didn't get _____.

    a. left   *b.* hurt   *c.* reduced   *d.* destroyed

4 I avoid drinking soft drinks that have a large _____ of sugar.

    a. loss   *b.* cost   *c.* waste   *d.* amount

Unit ★ 05

PLACES

A Connect each word to its correct definition.

1 to start to be seen • • **a.** layer

2 a large dry area with almost no plants • • **b.** reflect

3 a sheet of something that covers an area • • **c.** desert

4 to show the image of something in a mirror or water • • **d.** appear

B Write the word that has the opposite meaning of each word.

giant	heaven	thin	endless

1 hell : _____   2 tiny : _____

3 thick : _____   4 limited : _____

★ *The Salar de Uyuni*

Before Reading
What do you think a salt desert looks like?

Some people call it "a sea of salt" or "a white heaven." It is the Salar de Uyuni, the world's largest salt desert, and it's located in Bolivia, South America.

The Salar de Uyuni is famous for its unearthly
5 landscape. This white desert is situated at a height of 3,650 m, so it shines brightly under the sun. (①) And it seems endless. (②) That's the size of 1,500 soccer fields. (③) No wonder it looks like somewhere out of this world! (④) What's more, during the rainy season, even more magical scenery appears. The whole area becomes a giant mirror. A thin layer of
10 water on the ground reflects the sky clearly. It makes people feel like they're walking on the clouds.

_____(A)_____ The Salar de Uyuni was not always a salt desert. It used to be part of a large saltwater lake. However, the dry air of the Bolivian highlands caused all of the water to disappear over
15 time. This left 10 billion tons of salt on the land. As a result, this wonderful scenery was created!

READING COMPREHENSION

1 What is the passage mainly about?

   a. A strange place in space

   b. A large area covered with salt

   c. The great scenery on an island

   d. People living in a land of death

2 Where would the following sentence best fit?

> In fact, it takes up more than 10,000 km².

a. ①   *b.* ②   *c.* ③   *d.* ④

3 Why does the writer mention <u>a giant mirror</u>?

a. To show how big the place is
b. To explain how water reflects light
c. To describe the magical scenery of the desert
d. To express the feeling of walking on the clouds

4 How might people feel when they visit the Salar de Uyuni?

a. bored   *b.* amazed   *c.* confused   *d.* disappointed

5 What is the best choice for blank (A)?

a. Why is this salt desert popular?
b. What is so special about this place?
c. How was this amazing salt desert made?
d. Who thought of making this amazing place?

6 How did the water in the saltwater lake dry up?

_____

STRATEGIC SUMMARY

Fill in the blanks with the correct words.

The Salar de Uyuni is the world's largest salt _____. It is located at a height of 3,650 m. It is as large as 1,500 soccer fields and is covered in white salt. During the _____ season, something amazing happens. The whole area becomes a big _____. The water on the ground reflects the sky. This area used to be a giant saltwater _____. But the water disappeared and left all the salt behind.

> lake   view   desert   rainy   mirror

VOCABULARY REVIEW

A Complete the sentences with the words in the box. (Change the form if needed.)

scenery	height	billion	locate	leave

1 The plane flew at a _____ of 3,000 meters.

2 You can enjoy the beautiful _____ from the beach.

3 I spilled the grape juice, and it _____ a stain on the cloth.

4 The library is _____ in the center of town. It's easy to get there.

B Find the word that has a similar meaning to the underlined word.

1 Obesity can <u>cause</u> serious health problems.

    a. lead to   *b.* look for   *c.* care for   *d.* be good at

2 He heard an <u>unearthly</u> scream in the woods last night.

    a. loud   *b.* strange   *c.* common   *d.* friendly

C Choose the best word to complete each sentence.

1 The full moon was _____ brightly in the sky.

    a. going   *b.* shining   *c.* sinking   *d.* moving

2 When I clicked the button, the files _____ and I couldn't find them.

    a. disappeared   *b.* showed   *c.* existed   *d.* opened

3 She has _____ powers to see people's future.

    a. plain   *b.* typical   *c.* magical   *d.* dull

4 These noodles taste like the ones my mom _____ cook.

    a. seemed to   *b.* failed to   *c.* forgot to   *d.* used to

Unit ★ 06

LITERATURE

A Connect each word to its correct definition.

1 extremely good   •   • *a.* scratch

2 a person who investigates a crime   •   • *b.* excellent

3 a teacher at a university or college   •   • *c.* detective

4 a light cut on the surface of something   •   • *d.* professor

B Write the word that has a similar meaning to each word.

damage	happen	guess	return

1 harm : _____   *2* suppose : _____

3 come back : _____   *4* take place : _____

★ A Sherlock Holmes Story

Before Reading

Have you ever read a Sherlock Holmes story?

Sherlock Holmes is an excellent detective. One day, Hilton Soames, a professor at the College of St. Luke's, comes to see him. Professor Soames asks for help and explains what happened.

Tomorrow, there is an exam to decide who will receive a scholarship to the
5 college. So I looked over a copy of the test papers this afternoon. At four thirty, I put the papers on my desk and left the office for an appointment with a friend. When I returned an hour later, I saw a key inside the door. My servant had left it there by mistake.

I entered the office and noticed that
_____(A)_____. One page was on the floor, and another was on the table. Plus, I noticed a scratch on my table. I also found a broken *pencil lead next to the test papers. So I guess someone copied them in a hurry. I think you need to question the three students who will take the exam tomorrow. They are Giles Gilchrist, Daulat Ras, and Miles McLaren. They live in the same building where my office is.

If people find out about this incident, it will damage the reputation of the college. Please, Mr. Holmes, help me solve this problem quickly and in secret.

*pencil lead: the center part of a pencil used for writing

READING COMPREHENSION

1 What is the best title for the passage?

a. The Case of the Missing Servant
b. The Case of the Copied Test Papers
c. The Case of the Mysterious College
d. The Case of the Professor's Lost Key

2 Why did Professor Soames leave the office at four thirty?

   a. He had a plan to meet a friend.

   b. His servant had to clean his room.

   c. He had to attend a meeting about the exam.

   d. He went to a printing shop to get the test papers.

3 What is the best choice for blank (A)?

   a. the papers were gone

   b. someone's key was on the table

   c. there was a short note on my desk

   d. the papers were not where I had left them

4 Why does Professor Soames want to solve the problem quickly and secretly?

   Because if people find out about this problem, _____.

5 Which of the following best describes how Professor Soames feels?

   a. happy and proud   b. lonely and scared

   c. worried and nervous   d. excited and surprised

6 What is NOT true about Professor Soames?

   a. He will decide who will receive a scholarship.

   b. He found out someone was in his office.

   c. He thinks someone copied the test papers.

   d. He suspects one of his students.

STRATEGIC ORGANIZER

Fill in the blanks with the correct words.

A Sherlock Holmes Story

Case: Someone _____ the test papers in a professor's office.

Clues: Papers not in the _____ place
          A scratch on the table and _____ pencil lead

Suspects: Giles Gilchrist, Daulat Ras, and Miles McLaren
               They live in the _____ where the professor's
               office is.

_____

   entered   broken   original   copied   building

_____

★ ★ ★
VOCABULARY REVIEW

A Write the correct word next to its definition.

copy	secret	broken	scholarship	servant

1 information known to very few people: _____

2 damaged and separated into small pieces: _____

3 someone who cleans or cooks at someone else's home: _____

4 to make something that is similar or identical to another thing: _____

B Find the word that has a similar meaning to the underlined word.

1 The winner of this competition will <u>receive</u> 1,000 dollars.

   a. get   *b.* expect   *c.* improve   *d.* encourage

2 Although the <u>incident</u> happened long ago, I can still remember it vividly.

   a. disaster   *b.* story   *c.* event   *d.* change

C Choose the best word to complete each sentence.

1 Someone stole my purse, but I didn't _____ until today.

   a. allow   *b.* avoid   *c.* notice   *d.* decide

2 We need to take time to find a way to _____ this problem.

   a. offer   *b.* solve   *c.* agree   *d.* suggest

3 You have to call the hospital to make a(n) _____ with the doctor.

   a. profit   *b.* career   *c.* business   *d.* appointment

4 The police _____ the man, but he didn't admit his crime.

   a. chose   *b.* forgot   *c.* promised   *d.* questioned

Unit ★ 07

SPORTS

A Connect each word to its correct definition.

1 to have or own • • *a.* dot

2 a small round mark • • *b.* device

3 a machine or tool that does a particular job • • *c.* possess

4 playing or fighting against another person or group • • *d.* opposing

B Write the word that has the opposite meaning of each word.

| key | automatic | victory | divide |

1 defeat : _____

2 manual : _____

3 combine : _____

4 unimportant : _____

★ *Ball Possession in Soccer*

Have you ever wondered about the percentages shown on TV during soccer games? They refer to "ball possession." This is the amount of time a team has the ball.

_____ (A) _____ It's done with an automatic

5 analysis device. 16 cameras placed high in the stadium record different parts of the field and send the recordings to a computer. The computer sees the ball and players as dots, and it analyzes their movements. Then, it counts how long each team has the ball. (①) And it divides one team's time by the total time the ball is possessed. (②) It can make mistakes sometimes, such as

10 when two players fight for a ball. (③) So, it needs human support. (④) Two people also watch the game and add information that the device misses.

But why do we care about ball possession? Although it doesn't guarantee victory, it helps us know which team is more likely to win. Usually, more possession of the ball means that one team gives the opposing team

15 less time to score. This often plays a key role in winning the game. So

when you watch a soccer game, pay attention to ball possession to make the game more interesting!

READING COMPREHENSION

1 What is the best title for the passage?

a. What Is behind Soccer Ball Possession?
b. Advanced Technology in Soccer Games
c. Ball Possession: The Basic Rules of Soccer
d. Should We Trust Ball Possession in Soccer?

2 What is the best choice for blank (A)?

a. Who first made it?

b. What is its purpose?

c. Why is it important?

d. How is it measured?

3 What is NOT true about the analysis device?

a. It monitors 16 parts of the field.

b. Some of the cameras are set on the ground.

c. It includes cameras and a computer.

d. It sees the ball and players in the same way.

4 Where would the following sentence best fit?

However, the device isn't perfect.

a. ①

b. ②

c. ③

d. ④

5 Why is more possession of the ball considered important in winning a soccer game?

Because it means that _____ .

6 Write T if the statement is true or F if it's false.

1) Ball possession is the amount of time that a player has the ball.

2) The device measuring ball possession requires one person to assist.

STRATEGIC SUMMARY

Fill in the blanks with the correct words.

Ball possession is the _____ of time that each team has the ball during a soccer game. A special _____ is used to count how long each team has the ball. It has 16 cameras and a computer that analyzes the recordings. Two people help the device by _____ some missed information. Ball possession is important because it shows which team is more likely to win. A higher rate of possession usually plays a(n) _____ role in winning the game.

device	adding	key	field	amount

VOCABULARY REVIEW

★ ★ ★

A Complete the sentences with the words in the box. (Change the form if needed.)

care about	record	refer to	guarantee	score

1 He _____ two goals in the last World Cup Final.

2 Having a lot of money doesn't _____ happiness.

3 The earth is being destroyed. We should _____ the environment.

4 Yesterday, I _____ the TV show on a videotape so I can watch it again.

B Find the word that has a similar meaning to the underlined word.

1 I'm not able to do this alone. I need your support.

　　a. advice　　　*b.* decision　　　*c.* opinion　　　*d.* help

2 My mother placed her hand on my shoulder and said, "Cheer up!"

　　a. put　　　*b.* held　　　*c.* moved　　　*d.* washed

C Choose the best word to complete each sentence.

1 I'll _____ your foot to find your shoe size.

　　a. measure　　　*b.* count　　　*c.* calculate　　　*d.* add

2 He started his bakery with only a small _____ of money.

　　a. number　　　*b.* amount　　　*c.* height　　　*d.* group

3 I missed the end of the movie. I _____ how it ends.

　　a. decide　　　*b.* like　　　*c.* understand　　　*d.* wonder

4 If you don't eat right, you're more _____ to get sick.

　　a. successful　　　*b.* likely　　　*c.* open　　　*d.* impossible

Unit ★ 08

PEOPLE

A Connect each word to its correct definition.

1 not able to see •

2 a device for playing music •

3 several and of different types •

4 to learn something completely •

• *a.* blind

• *b.* master

• *c.* various

• *d.* instrument

B Write the word that has a similar meaning to each word.

surgery	talent	recognize	shortly

1 gift : _____

2 soon : _____

3 notice : _____

4 operation : _____

★ *Stevie Wonder*

Stevie Wonder is one of the world's best-known musicians. You may have seen him singing on stage wearing sunglasses. Though he's been blind since
5 shortly after birth, he never let this discourage him from becoming a musician. He overcame the difficulties of blindness with his love for music.

① As a young boy, he showed great interest in music and learned it naturally. ② He mastered various instruments like the piano
10 and the harmonica before he was ten. ③ Many musicians like playing the guitar better than the piano. ④ Soon, Motown Records recognized his talent and made him a singer. When he was just thirteen, his album *Fingertips* became a number one hit. Since then, he has had more than 30 U.S. top ten hits and won 25 Grammy Awards.

Stevie is not just a great musician. He is also _____(A)_____. Once, he tried to have eye surgery to see his children. Unfortunately, he couldn't get the surgery because his eyes weren't in good condition. Also, he shows his love for his children through his music. One of his most popular songs, "Isn't She Lovely," is about his first daughter, Aisha. Fans love Stevie for both his music and his character.

READING COMPREHENSION

1 **What is the best title for the passage?**

   a. Stevie Wonder's Secret Wish

   b. The Success Story of a Poor Singer

   c. A Singer's Love for Music and Family

   d. See the World through Your Inner Eye

2 How couldn't his blindness stop Stevie Wonder from becoming a singer?

_____

3 Which sentence is NOT needed in the passage?

    a. ①   *b.* ②   *c.* ③   *d.* ④

4 What is NOT true about Stevie Wonder?

    a. He was positive about his disability.

    b. He learned to play instruments at the age of 13.

    c. His album *Fingertips* was very successful.

    d. He has won more than 20 Grammy Awards.

5 What is the best choice for blank (A)?

    a. a good actor   *b.* a loving father

    c. a famous writer   *d.* an excellent producer

6 Why did Stevie Wonder try to have surgery on his eyes?

    a. He wanted to see his children.

    b. He felt serious pain in his eyes.

    c. He hoped to show a new image to his fans.

    d. He thought it would help him perform better on stage.

STRATEGIC ORGANIZER

Fill in the blanks with the correct words.

Stevie Wonder

As a musician
- He learned music at a young age despite his _____.
- He became one of the most _____ musicians in America.

As a father
- He tried to have eye _____ to see his kids.
- He shows his _____ for his children in his songs.

    love   surgery   popular   blindness   instruments

★ ★ ★
VOCABULARY REVIEW

A Write the correct word next to its definition.

hit	stage	award	musician	blindness

1 an area where an actor or singer performs: _____

2 someone who plays or writes music as a job: _____

3 something like a song, film, or play that is successful: _____

4 a prize given to someone for what he or she has done: _____

B Find the word that has the opposite meaning of the underlined word.

1 It is a <u>well-known</u> fact that you and Jamie are good friends.

    a. fake   *b.* able   *c.* truthful   *d.* unfamiliar

2 <u>Unfortunately</u>, our team lost the game.

    a. Quickly   *b.* Luckily   *c.* Surprisingly   *d.* Interestingly

C Choose the best word to complete each sentence.

1 The customer expressed _____ in the red T-shirt on the wall.

    a. ability   *b.* interest   *c.* condition   *d.* performance

2 Unlike his brother, Mike has a very cheerful and outgoing _____.

    a. place   *b.* tradition   *c.* character   *d.* instrument

3 The government has increased the price of cigarettes to _____ smoking.

    a. include   *b.* improve   *c.* promote   *d.* discourage

4 Greg _____ his injury and became the best player on the team.

    a. limited   *b.* suggested   *c.* overcame   *d.* expressed

Unit ★ 09

FOOD

A Connect each word to its correct definition.

1 a large group of people ● ● *a.* prove

2 an illness of people or animals ● ● *b.* crowd

3 to think or believe something will happen ● ● *c.* expect

4 to show that something is true by providing evidence ● ● *d.* disease

B Write the word that has the opposite meaning of each word.

harmful	rich	prevent	produce

1 low : _____ *2* safe : _____

3 cause : _____ *4* consume : _____

★ *Tomatoes*

Before Reading

Have you wondered when we started to eat tomatoes as food?

Every year, about 120 million tons of tomatoes are produced worldwide. People all over the world enjoy eating tomatoes! But, when tomatoes were brought to America in the 19th century, people _____(A)_____.

5 Many people thought they were very harmful. That's because there were rumors that poisonous substances in tomatoes would turn the blood into acid.

So how did people come to start eating tomatoes? According to legend, a man named Robert Gibbon Johnson proved that tomatoes are safe to eat. He ate a basket of tomatoes in front of a crowd. The people expected him to get ill and die, but he didn't. So people started to eat tomatoes!

Unlike in the past, people today like tomatoes because they're very healthy. Tomatoes have something called lycopene. ① It helps prevent heart disease, high blood pressure, and even cancer. ② Tomatoes also have a lot of vitamin E, which keeps your skin beautiful. ③ Vegetable oils, such as sunflower and corn oils, are also rich in vitamin E. ④ So tomatoes are used in a lot of foods today. These include ketchup, pasta sauce, juice, and pizza. Aren't tomatoes amazing?

READING COMPREHENSION

1 What is the best title for the passage?

a. Healthy Food All over the World

b. Robert Gibbon Johnson's Favorite Food

c. How Tomatoes Were Introduced to America

d. Tomatoes: From a Misunderstood Food to a Healthy Food

2 What is the best choice for blank (A)?

    a. were dying to eat them

    b. were worried about eating them

    c. didn't know if they were fruits or vegetables

    d. confused them with another poisonous plant

3 Why did Americans in the 19th century believe tomatoes were dangerous?

_____

4 What is the 2nd paragraph mainly about?

    a. How tomatoes were cooked in the past

    b. An event that led to people starting to eat tomatoes

    c. The reason why tomatoes are not popular in America

    d. A famous person who first brought tomatoes to America

5 What is NOT mentioned as a benefit of tomatoes?

    a. Keeping the heart healthy

    b. Maintaining normal blood pressure

    c. Helping the stomach digest food

    d. Keeping skin beautiful

6 Which sentence is NOT needed in the passage?

    a. ①   *b.* ②   *c.* ③   *d.* ④

STRATEGIC SUMMARY

Fill in the blanks with the correct words.

Tomatoes were not always as _____ as they are today. When they were brought to America, people thought they were _____. But Robert Gibbon Johnson showed people that they are okay to eat. Since then, people have enjoyed tomatoes. One reason for this is that they're very _____. They have many things that are good for our bodies. That's why we see them in so many _____ today.

> foods   disease   healthy   popular   poisonous

★ ★ ★
VOCABULARY REVIEW

A Complete the sentences with the words in the box. (Change the form if needed.)

legend	past	skin	include	worldwide

1 This story is a(n) _____ that has been passed down in our village.

2 If you stay under the sun for a long time, it will burn your _____.

3 Women only wore skirts in the _____, but now they also wear pants.

4 Study of a foreign language _____ reading, listening, speaking, and writing.

B Find the word that has a similar meaning to the underlined word.

1 She covered herself with a blanket to keep warm.

    a. stay   *b.* turn   *c.* help   *d.* change

2 The girl named Jenny is Lisa's sister.

    a. brought   *b.* followed   *c.* shown   *d.* called

C Choose the best word to complete each sentence.

1 He was taken to the hospital after eating a(n) _____ mushroom.

    a. safe   *b.* positive   *c.* poisonous   *d.* effective

2 One of the best ways to lower blood _____ is regular exercise.

    a. pressure   *b.* acid   *c.* substance   *d.* rate

3 Smoking can cause lung _____.

    a. effort   *b.* result   *c.* mistake   *d.* cancer

4 There's been a strange _____ going around about the actor recently.

    a. mark   *b.* rumor   *c.* speech   *d.* cold

Unit ★ 10

ECONOMY

A Connect each word to its correct definition.

1 doing something secretly · · *a.* aim

2 a result that you want to achieve · · *b.* hang out

3 to say that something is good or useful · · *c.* undercover

4 to spend a lot of time in a particular place · · *d.* recommend

B Write the word that has a similar meaning to each word.

latest	trust	friendly	advertise

1 kind : _____   *2* believe : _____

3 recent : _____   *4* promote : _____

★ *Undercover Marketing*

Before Reading
What do companies do to sell more of their products?

A tourist asks you to take a picture. When you agree, she hands you the latest model of a popular digital camera. Then she shows you how it works and tells you how much she likes it. Is she really a tourist? Actually, she is advertising the camera using undercover marketing.

5   Undercover marketing is a kind of _____(A)_____ marketing. Companies pay actors or friendly people to use their products and talk about them. They do it in places where consumers hang out, such as malls. But they never explain their purpose or force you to buy anything. Their aim is to let people know about the products in a natural way so that they'll want to buy 10 them.

    These days, this kind of marketing is often more effective than regular commercials. That's because many people don't trust what commercials say and don't pay attention to them. Also, this marketing strategy makes it possible to get people's attention through _____(B)_____.
15 People who tried a product write reviews and recommend it to their friends. This works because people are more likely to trust what their friends say. Now that you know what undercover marketing is, you'll recognize lots of examples around you!

READING COMPREHENSION

1 **What is the passage mainly about?**

  a. The secret of a successful marketer

  b. Marketing that consumers don't notice

  c. A unique idea to make on-site sales possible

  d. A type of newly invented online marketing plan

2 How does the writer introduce the topic?

a. By advertising the latest camera model

b. By describing various methods of advertising

c. By giving an example of undercover marketing

d. By explaining the strong points of undercover marketing

3 What is the best choice for blank (A)?

a. green

b. online

c. secret

d. international

4 What is the best choice for blank (B)?

a. print ads

b. official information

c. word-of-mouth recommendations

d. critical reviews about the companies

5 Why do recommendations from friends work well?

_____

6 Write T if the statement is true or F if it's false.

1) Undercover marketers can be found in shopping centers.

2) Commercials are considered the best way to advertise products.

STRATEGIC SUMMARY

Fill in the blanks with the correct words.

Undercover marketing is marketing strategy that consumers don't realize. It involves telling consumers about products in a(n) _____ way. Companies use this marketing because many people don't _____ what commercials say. Undercover marketing is _____ in getting people's attention. That's because people can talk about the products to their friends. This _____ works well because people tend to believe their friends' words.

| regular | trust | natural | effective | word of mouth |

★ ★ ★
VOCABULARY REVIEW

A Complete the sentences with the words in the box. (Change the form if needed.)

| consumer | purpose | commercial | product | marketing |

1 What is the _____ of your visit to America?

2 The company did a survey to find out what _____ want.

3 John found a defect in the _____ and complained about it.

4 I bought a new kind of shampoo after watching a _____ on TV.

B Find the word that has the opposite meaning of the underlined word.

1 I suggested we watch a movie this weekend, and she agreed.

   a. refused   *b.* believed   *c.* expressed   *d.* depended

2 It is not possible to finish all the work by the end of this week.

   a. able   *b.* unfortunate   *c.* hopeful   *d.* unlikely

C Choose the best word to complete each sentence.

1 Chris was still in bed, so his mother _____ him to get up.

   a. aimed   *b.* forced   *c.* reduced   *d.* improved

2 How much should I _____ for renting two bicycles?

   a. pay   *b.* reward   *c.* promote   *d.* recognize

3 I got the autograph of the main _____ after the play finished.

   a. actor   *b.* cause   *c.* effect   *d.* product

4 The treatment was very _____, and he got better quickly.

   a. terrible   *b.* negative   *c.* natural   *d.* effective

Unit ★ 11

FESTIVALS

A Connect each word to its correct definition.

1 in a respectful way • • **a.** pour

2 a building where people worship a god • • **b.** politely

3 to make a liquid flow out of a container • • **c.** temple

4 to do something special for an important occasion • • **d.** celebrate

B Write the word that has a similar meaning to each word.

wet	luck	wish	symbolize

1 hope : _____ **2** moist : _____

3 fortune : _____ **4** represent : _____

★ *Songkran*

People all around the world celebrate the New Year in their own way. Some make wishes for the coming year. Others eat special food for good luck. In Thailand, everyone _____ (A) _____ for the New Year!

Thai people celebrate the New Year with the Songkran festival for three to ten days in mid-April. It's not in January

10 because April 13th is New Year's Day in the Thai calendar. Usually, Songkran is a time for making everything clean and new again. (①) So people clean out their homes or visit a temple to clear their minds at this time. (②) People throw water at each other, even at strangers, during Songkran. (③) They use water guns, hoses, and buckets — just like in a water fight! (④) It's really

15 fun, and the cool water is very refreshing during the hot April weather in Thailand.

So why do people throw water? It symbolizes washing off all misfortunes and welcoming the New Year with a fresh new start. Traditionally, people politely poured a bowl of water on their family or

20 friends. But then the mood became more festive, and people started to enjoy playful water fights. If you're still curious about Songkran, how about visiting Thailand for it?

READING COMPREHENSION

1 What is the best title for the passage?

a. The Sad Story behind Songkran

b. New Year Traditions around the World

c. Songkran: A Water Fight for the New Year

d. Thailand's Culture of Respecting One's Family

2 What is the best choice for blank (A)?

    a. gets totally wet

    b. sings traditional songs

    c. enjoys the festival of lights

    d. throws flowers at each other

3 Why do people in Thailand celebrate the New Year in April?

_____

4 Where would the following sentence best fit?

> But the most famous part of Songkran is the throwing of water.

    a. ①   *b.* ②   *c.* ③   *d.* ④

5 What is the 3rd paragraph mainly about? (Choose two.)

    a. The meaning of throwing water

    b. The most famous festival in Thailand

    c. How a Songkran tradition has changed

    d. The importance of respecting each other

6 What is NOT true according to the passage?

    a. Songkran lasts for three to ten days.

    b. Thai people clean out their homes during Songkran.

    c. A variety of things are used to throw water during the festival.

    d. In the past, water wasn't used during Songkran.

STRATEGIC SUMMARY

Fill in the blanks with the correct words.

In April, people in Thailand _____ the New Year with a festival called Songkran. During this festival, people usually _____ their homes or visit temples. But the most famous event is the _____ of water, which represents washing off bad fortune and welcoming the New Year. Originally, people _____ water on their family and friends. But then the mood became more festive, and people started to enjoy playful water fights.

> clean   water   poured   celebrate   throwing

★ ★ ★
VOCABULARY REVIEW

A Complete the sentences with the words in the box. (Change the form if needed.)

bucket	wash off	throw	misfortune	stranger

1 I asked them to _____ the stains on my white shirt.

2 She is naturally shy, so it is not easy for her to talk to a _____.

3 Larry had the _____ of breaking his leg before the tournament.

4 He didn't turn off the faucet, and the water spilled out of the _____.

B Find the word that has the opposite meaning of the underlined word.

1 Lemonade is a good, refreshing drink during a hot summer day.

   a. tiring   *b.* amusing   *c.* cooling   *d.* relaxing

2 You can enjoy the beautiful view on top of the mountain.

   a. try   *b.* hate   *c.* bring   *d.* finish

C Choose the best word to complete each sentence.

1 Nobody wanted to go out because of the cold _____.

   a. heat   *b.* increase   *c.* weather   *d.* darkness

2 You should _____ the doctor for a checkup.

   a. visit   *b.* work   *c.* learn   *d.* discover

3 Originally, March was the first month in the Roman _____.

   a. history   *b.* culture   *c.* calendar   *d.* technology

4 The music perfectly fits the _____ of the party.

   a. mind   *b.* mood   *c.* matter   *d.* experience

Unit ★ 12

PSYCHOLOGY

A Connect each word to its correct definition.

1 relating to seeing or sight •   • *a.* bowl

2 to eat more than your body needs •   • *b.* visual

3 a round, deep dish that holds liquid or food •   • *c.* overeat

4 the study of something to find new information •   • *d.* research

B Write the word that has the opposite meaning of each word.

add	bottom	hungry	secretly

1 top : _____   2 full : _____

3 reduce : _____   4 openly : _____

★ Why People Overeat

Before Reading
When do you think you overeat?

What causes you to overeat? You may think you overeat only when you're really hungry. But this isn't always true. Research shows that visual signs have a bigger effect on overeating than hunger. In other

5 words, what you see can determine how much you eat.

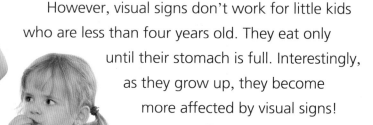

    In a test, two groups of people were asked to eat soup until they felt full. But the soup was served to each group in different bowls. (①) People in group A had soup in a regular bowl. (②) People in group B ate soup from a special bowl that had a hidden tube at the bottom.

10 (③) Therefore, group B's soup decreased at a slower speed than normal. (④) The results were interesting. People in group B said they were full after eating 73% more than those in group A. The reason for this was that people in group B saw no visual sign of eating a lot. _____ (A) while they were eating!

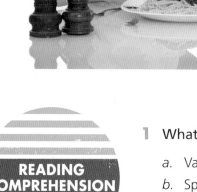

15   However, visual signs don't work for little kids who are less than four years old. They eat only until their stomach is full. Interestingly, as they grow up, they become more affected by visual signs!

READING COMPREHENSION

1 **What is the passage mainly about?**

  a. Various ways to make people eat less

  b. Special bowls for people who are on a diet

  c. A study showing how much people love eating

  d. Something that controls how much people eat

2 Where would the following sentence best fit?

> It was used to secretly add more soup to the bowl.

a. ①   *b.* ②   *c.* ③   *d.* ④

3 What is the best choice for blank (A)?

a. The soup was the same color

b. Nobody told them they were having less soup

c. They didn't know that they were using bigger spoons

d. The amount of soup in the bowl didn't go down very much

4 What can be inferred from the 2nd paragraph?

a. People in group B didn't have good vision.

b. The goal of the test was to see who could eat the most.

c. A regular bowl would have made people in group B eat less.

d. People in group A had smaller stomachs than those in group B.

5 Why aren't children under four years old affected by visual signs?

_____

6 Write T if the statement is true or F if it's false.

1) Hunger is not the only reason we overeat.

2) In the test, the taste of the soup affected how much people ate.

STRATEGIC SUMMARY

Fill in the blanks with the correct words.

People don't _____ only because they're hungry. People are actually more influenced by visual signs. This was shown in a test done on two groups. People in group A ate soup from a(n) _____ bowl until they felt full. People in group B also ate until they felt full, but more soup was secretly _____ to their bowls. Thus, the soup didn't _____ as quickly from their bowls. The result was that they ate more without feeling full. But these visual signs don't affect very young children.

> added   overeat   regular   hunger   disappear

★ ★ ★
VOCABULARY REVIEW

A Complete the sentences with the words in the box. (Change the form if needed.)

sign	tube	hunger	stomach	grow up

1 Liquid travels through this long, thin _____.

2 Can you give me something to eat? I'm dying of _____.

3 My _____ was upset after eating lots of ice cream last night.

4 The twins lived with their grandparents while they were _____.

B Find the word that has a similar meaning to the underlined word.

1 Saturday is a regular working day for me.

    a. fun   *b.* normal   *c.* special   *d.* unlucky

2 The new teaching method positively affected students' grades.

    a. decreased   *b.* prevented   *c.* influenced   *d.* exchanged

C Choose the best word to complete each sentence.

1 Breakfast is _____ between 8:30 and 10:30 a.m.

    a. rose   *b.* served   *c.* caused   *d.* decided

2 The sailors found _____ treasure on a desert island.

    a. grown   *b.* opposing   *c.* hired   *d.* hidden

3 The _____ for the delay was bad weather.

    a. effort   *b.* comparison   *c.* reason   *d.* freedom

4 The express train is traveling at a(n) _____ of 300 kilometers per hour.

    a. goal   *b.* speed   *c.* matter   *d.* amount

Unit ★ 13
SCIENCE

VOCABULARY PREVIEW

A Connect each word to its correct definition.

1 a mixture of gases around the earth • • *a.* object

2 to say something will happen in the future • • *b.* launch

3 to send something into the air or into space • • *c.* predict

4 a thing that can be seen or touched but isn't alive • • *d.* atmosphere

B Write the word that has the opposite meaning of each word.

modern	impossible	send	improve

1 likely : _____

2 receive : _____

3 ancient : _____

4 worsen : _____

★ *Satellites*

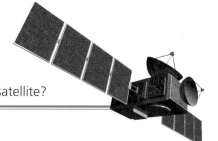

Before Reading
Can you think of anything that uses a satellite?

Right now, there are thousands of objects flying over your head. They're not birds or airplanes — think higher. They're satellites that are sent into space and travel in circles around the earth!

The first satellite was Sputnik I, which was launched by the Soviet Union
5 in 1957. It was shaped like a ball and it weighed just 83.6 kg. Its purpose was to learn about the earth's atmosphere. After this, satellite technology greatly improved. But for years, it belonged only to the military.

Recently, however, satellite technologies have been created for everyone to use. _____(A)_____, satellites now help many people drive.
10 (①) There is a special group of satellites that work with the *GPS device in your car. (②) These satellites track your location as you drive and send you directions. (③) This is possible because satellites with special cameras are used to watch and predict weather changes on the earth. (④) And satellite

television uses satellites, of course. TV stations send signals to their satellites. These signals bounce off the satellites and travel to your television. It is impossible to imagine our modern lives without satellites, isn't it?

*GPS: Global Positioning System

READING COMPREHENSION

1 What is the passage mainly about?

a. The invention of satellites
b. The advantages of modern technology
c. The various uses of satellite technology
d. How the first artificial satellite was born

2 Why did the Soviet Union launch Sputnik I in 1957?

They launched it _____.

3 What can be inferred from the underlined part?

　　a. Only the military was interested in satellite technology.

　　b. Early satellite technology was developed for military use.

　　c. Less developed technology was used in the private sector.

　　d. It was the military that opened satellite technology to everyone.

4 What is the best choice for blank (A)?

　　a. Instead

　　c. In addition

　　b. However

　　d. For example

5 Where would the following sentence best fit?

> Satellites also tell us what the weather will be like tomorrow.

　　a. ①　　　　　*b.* ②　　　　　*c.* ③　　　　　*d.* ④

6 What is NOT mentioned as a recent use of satellites?

　　a. Finding directions

　　c. Watching satellite TV

　　b. Predicting the weather

　　d. Sending radio signals

STRATEGIC ORGANIZER

Fill in the blanks with the correct words.

Satellites — Devices in _____ that circle around the earth

The uses of the first satellites
- Sputnik I was used to study the earth's _____.
- Only the military used satellite technology.

The uses of satellites today
- GPS satellites help us while _____.
- Satellites with cameras predict the _____.
- Satellite television depends on satellite signals.

```
driving    purpose    space    weather    atmosphere
```

★ ★ ★
VOCABULARY REVIEW

A Complete the sentences with the words in the box. (Change the form if needed.)

bounce	military	weather	weigh	location

1 My laptop computer is not heavy. It only _____ 1 kg.

2 Mike tried to catch the ball, but it _____ off his glove.

3 Would you mind showing me our exact _____ on this map?

4 All male citizens of the Republic of Korea are required to serve in the _____.

B Find the word that has a similar meaning to the underlined word.

1 It is a well-known fact that light travels faster than sound.

 a. flies   *b.* walks   *c.* moves   *d.* looks around

2 There have been many traffic accidents recently.

 a. lately   *b.* lastly   *c.* early   *d.* nearly

C Choose the best word to complete each sentence.

1 Can you give me _____ to the subway station?

 a. orders   *b.* objects   *c.* directions   *d.* suggestions

2 Do you know who this dog _____ to? I'm trying to find its owner.

 a. refers   *b.* points   *c.* looks   *d.* belongs

3 I can't make a call from my cellphone. The _____ is too weak.

 a. letter   *b.* package   *c.* signal   *d.* check

4 The forecasters could _____ the storm by using radar.

 a. track   *b.* lack   *c.* pack   *d.* attack

Unit ★ 14

SOCIETY

A Connect each word to its correct definition.

1 relating to the law · · *a.* legal

2 to ask for money for something · · *b.* talent

3 a natural ability to do something well · · *c.* charge

4 a person whose job requires a special skill · · *d.* professional

B Write the word that has a similar meaning to each word.

normally	offer	set up	employee

1 provide : _____   *2* install : _____

3 worker : _____   *4* usually : _____

★ *Pro Bono*

Before Reading

Have you ever done volunteer work? If you have, what did you do?

If you have a special talent or skill, you can use it to help others! This is called "pro bono" work. The Latin term "pro bono" means "for the public

5 good." Pro bono workers do the same services that they normally do at their jobs. But the difference is that they do not charge anything.

The idea of pro bono work began in the legal world in the 1970s. (①)
10 Many poor people couldn't get legal help because they couldn't pay for a lawyer. (②) Soon, many people realized that pro bono work was helpful for society. (③) Later, other professionals like doctors and builders began doing pro bono work, too. (④)

These days, pro bono work _____(A)_____. Many big
15 companies organize pro bono work so that their employees have chances to help others. For example, some information technology companies send their workers to schools. There, they help set up computers for the students. Since big companies started to get involved, pro bono work has become more and more popular. So now, more people are doing it, and this is improving our
20 society!

READING COMPREHENSION

1 What is the best title for the passage?

　　a. The Joy of Volunteer Work
　　b. Why Does Society Need Laws?
　　c. Pro Bono: Donating Your Talent
　　d. Pro Bono: The Government's Power

2 What does the Latin term "pro bono" mean in English?

_____

3 Where would the following sentence best fit?

So some lawyers started offering free services for the poor.

a. ①   b. ②   c. ③   d. ④

4 What is the best choice for blank (A)?

a. is done in the legal world

b. isn't only done by individuals

c. isn't as popular as in the past

d. has helped many poor people

5 What is the 3rd paragraph mainly about?

a. Types of pro bono work   b. The history of pro bono work

c. The spread of pro bono work   d. The benefits of pro bono work

6 Write T if the statement is true or F if it's false.

_1)_ Pro bono workers perform professional services for free.

_2)_ Many big companies do pro bono work for their employees.

STRATEGIC ORGANIZER

Fill in the blanks with the correct words.

Pro Bono

In the past
- It was started by _____ who offered legal help for free.
- Other _____ saw the benefits and started doing it, too.

Today
- Companies have their _____ do pro bono work.
- It has become more _____ since big companies got involved.

skill   lawyers   popular   employees   professionals

★ ★ ★
VOCABULARY REVIEW

A Complete the sentences with the words in the box. (Change the form if needed.)

builder	public	popular	realize	lawyer

1 Coffee is one of the most _____ drinks in the world.

2 When I talked to him, I _____ how much he loved me.

3 The program focuses on _____ health issues, such as smoking.

4 Sue attends law school. She wants to be a _____ in the future.

B Find the word that has the opposite meaning of the underlined word.

1 This herbal tea will be <u>helpful</u> for your stomachache.

    a. kind   *b.* useless   *c.* valuable   *d.* convenient

2 Men and women should recognize their <u>differences</u> and respect each other.

    a. changes   *b.* materials   *c.* directions   *d.* similarities

C Choose the best word to complete each sentence.

1 She applied for the advanced French class to _____ her French.

    a. help   *b.* improve   *c.* protect   *d.* continue

2 Sam is offering his _____ as a shuttle bus driver.

    a. jobs   *b.* money   *c.* services   *d.* licenses

3 This work is so simple that it doesn't require any professional _____.

    a. skills   *b.* export   *c.* demand   *d.* payment

4 Brian will _____ a baseball club to play baseball with other students.

    a. work   *b.* notice   *c.* prohibit   *d.* organize

Unit ★ 15

ENTERTAINMENT

A Connect each word to its correct definition.

1 the words of a song • • **a.** lyrics

2 the script for a movie • • **b.** musical

3 the form of energy carried by wires • • **c.** electricity

4 a play that uses singing and dancing to tell a story • • **d.** screenplay

B Write the word that has a similar meaning to each word.

| move | upset | award | attract |

1 draw : _____ 2 prize : _____

3 unhappy : _____ 4 impress : _____

★ Billy Elliot the Musical

Dear Diary,

Today I went to see *Billy Elliot the Musical* with my family. It has attracted millions of people around the world since it first opened in London in 2005. I heard it had won many awards, so I couldn't wait to see it.

5   *Billy Elliot the Musical* is based on the movie of the same title. The screenplay and song lyrics were written by Lee Hall. (①) The musical focuses on a boy named Billy. (②) His father wants him to be a boxer, but Billy realizes he wants to be a ballet dancer. (③) But later, he begins to understand Billy and helps him achieve his dream. (④) Everything about the

10 musical was awesome. I especially liked the actor who played Billy. Though he was a young boy just like me, his dancing skills were great!

    While I was watching this musical, I was greatly moved by Billy's passion for dancing. When Billy is asked "What does it feel like when you are dancing?," he starts to sing "Electricity." "Like electricity, electricity. Sparks

15 inside of me. And I'm free, I'm free." When I heard these words, I could feel how happy he was when he danced.

READING COMPREHENSION

1 What is the passage mainly about?

   a. A day at the cinema in London

   b. A musical about a boy who loves ballet

   c. An audition for a role in a world-famous musical

   d. A field trip to meet a young actor from a musical

2 What can be inferred from the underlined sentence?

    a. The musical is performed illegally.

    b. The movie was also directed by Lee Hall.

    c. The movie came out before the musical did.

    d. The running time of the musical is the same as that of the movie.

3 What is NOT true about *Billy Elliot the Musical*?

    a. People first saw it in London.

    b. It has won lots of awards.

    c. Lee Hall wrote the song lyrics for it.

    d. It includes performances with animals.

4 Where would the following sentence best fit?

At first, his father is upset by this.

    a. ①   *b.* ②   *c.* ③   *d.* ④

5 Why did the writer especially like the actor who played Billy?

    _____

6 Why does the writer mention the song "Electricity"?

    a. To tell Billy's childhood story

    b. To describe the difficulties Billy had

    c. To explain why Billy gave up boxing

    d. To show Billy's great love for dancing

STRATEGIC SUMMARY

Fill in the blanks with the correct words.

The writer went to see *Billy Elliot the Musical*. This musical is based on a _____ and tells the story of a young boy named Billy. His father expects him to become a boxer, but Billy wants to be a _____ dancer. Eventually, he achieves his _____. The writer was especially impressed by the dancing ability of the actor. The most memorable part was Billy's performance of the song "Electricity," which shows his _____ for dancing.

skill   dream   movie   ballet   passion

★ ★ ★
VOCABULARY REVIEW

A Complete the sentences with the words in the box. (Change the form if needed.)

title	million	spark	focus	achieve

1 Pablo Picasso _____ great success as an artist.

2 This room is so noisy that I can't _____ on my studies.

3 A lot of _____ came out of the old TV, and it caught on fire.

4 Her novel was published under the _____ *Pride and Prejudice*.

B Find the word that has the opposite meaning of the underlined word.

1 The view from the top of the Eiffel Tower was <u>awesome</u>.

   a. great   *b.* poor   *c.* shocking   *d.* pleasant

2 The class is dismissed. Now you are <u>free</u> to leave.

   a. busy   *b.* cheap   *c.* allowed   *d.* restricted

C Choose the best word to complete each sentence.

1 People will be shocked to know that the film is _____ on a true story.

   a. based   *b.* possible   *c.* interested   *d.* unbelievable

2 He _____ his mistake after a long time, but it was too late.

   a. made   *b.* enjoyed   *c.* expected   *d.* realized

3 We hope that you feel the joy and _____ of this performance.

   a. passion   *b.* discount   *c.* regret   *d.* climate

4 I loved this restaurant so much that I couldn't _____ to come back.

   a. afford   *b.* choose   *c.* promise   *d.* wait

Unit ★ 16

HUMAN BODY

★ ──── **VOCABULARY PREVIEW** ──── ★

A Connect each word to its correct definition.

1 feeling comfortable and not worried •   • *a.* injure

2 in a way that is connected to one's body •   • *b.* create

3 to make something that didn't exist before •   • *c.* relaxed

4 to hurt and cause damage to someone's body •   • *d.* physically

B Write the word that has a similar meaning to each word.

depressed	occur	tough	exercise

1 difficult : _____   *2* gloomy : _____

3 work out : _____   *4* happen : _____

★ *Runner's High*

Running is hard exercise. Therefore, you may think running for a long time would be harder and more painful. However, runners say that
5 they actually feel less tired and even happy when they run for a long time. That's because their bodies create endorphins, the hormones that make us feel good.
10 While these hormones are active, runners feel great both physically and mentally. This experience is called a "runner's high"!

To feel a runner's high, people must run for longer than 30 minutes.
15 (①) And they should be relaxed and comfortable. (②) So people in a tough race don't usually experience it. (③) Skiers, swimmers, tennis players, and other athletes can experience this feeling, too. (④) When the runner's high begins, they feel wonderful and believe they can keep exercising or playing forever.

20 However, you should be careful not to _____(A)_____.
A runner's high comes and goes quickly. So some people exercise too much to feel it more often. Far from making them healthy, this can injure their muscles. Also, it can make them feel depressed when they can't exercise. So, remember this: Too much is as bad as too little.

READING COMPREHENSION

1 What is the best title for the passage?

   a. How to Be a Fast Runner
   b. The Importance of Regular Exercise
   c. Two Different Sides of a Runner's High
   d. A Runner's High: A Reward for Race Winners

2 How do runners feel when endorphins are active?

_____

3 Where would the following sentence best fit?

| A runner's high doesn't only occur while running, though. |

a. ①   *b.* ②   *c.* ③   *d.* ④

4 What is the best choice for blank (A)?

a. miss this moment

b. get addicted to this feeling

c. be relaxed while exercising

d. run for less than 30 minutes

5 Who is giving FALSE information about a runner's high?

a. Brian: It occurs after running for more than 30 minutes.

b. Lucy: A tennis player can experience it.

c. Jenny: It makes people want to stop exercising.

b. Martin: It lasts only for a short time.

6 Write T if the statement is true or F if it's false.

1) People can feel a runner's high while running or playing sports.

2) The more often you feel a runner's high, the healthier you become.

STRATEGIC SUMMARY

Fill in the blanks with the correct words.

Sometimes, runners get a feeling of great _____ while running. It's called a runner's high, and it comes from _____ created by the body. Relaxed running for over 30 minutes can produce the feeling. Other athletes can also _____ it. They say it makes them never want to stop. However, you must be careful because a runner's high can be _____. This can harm your health physically and mentally.

| tough   addictive   hormones   happiness   experience |

★ ★ ★
VOCABULARY REVIEW

A Complete the sentences with the words in the box. (Change the form if needed.)

runner	painful	forever	mentally	comfortable

1 I suffered a _____ neck injury in a car accident.

2 This bed is so _____ that I fall asleep in it right away.

3 The two _____ reached the finish line at the same time.

4 He was _____ ill, so he couldn't judge what was right or wrong.

B Find the word that has the opposite meaning of the underlined word.

1 The virus is usually <u>active</u> at low temperatures.

   a. immobile   *b.* excited   *c.* actual   *d.* general

2 Sophia felt <u>tired</u> after working for hours without a break.

   a. lively   *b.* bored   *c.* friendly   *d.* interested

C Choose the best word to complete each sentence.

1 David does push-ups to build his arm _____.

   a. skills   *b.* effects   *c.* results   *d.* muscles

2 In this program, you can _____ ancient lifestyles.

   a. teach   *b.* require   *c.* improve   *d.* experience

3 Lionel Messi is the best _____ on Argentina's soccer team.

   a. activity   *b.* athlete   *c.* function   *d.* employer

4 Dave plays video games every day. I think he's _____ to them.

   a. relieved   *b.* anxious   *c.* addicted   *d.* disappointed

Unit ★ 17
EDUCATION

A Connect each word to its correct definition.

1 a test to find out something • • *a.* lesson

2 something that students learn • • *b.* demand

3 to ask for something very strongly • • *c.* perform

4 to do something such as a job or a piece of work • • *d.* experiment

B Write the word that has the opposite meaning of each word.

smart	randomly	remember	beginning

1 end : _____   *2* forget : _____

3 foolish : _____   *4* in order : _____

① Imagine you're a teacher. ② If you tell your students they're not smart, they'll probably do badly in class. ③ But, if you tell them that they're geniuses, they'll probably do well. ④ Taking notes in class helps students remember their lesson better. This situation describes what is
5　called the Pygmalion effect. The Pygmalion effect says that people given _____(A)_____ perform well, and people given _____(B)_____ perform poorly.

This effect was shown in an experiment at a California elementary school in 1966. At the beginning of the experiment, researchers randomly

10　selected a few students from one class. They told their teacher that these students were smarter than their classmates. Surprisingly, they found the randomly selected students actually got higher grades at the end of the experiment.

Why did this happen? The teacher expected them to do better. He paid extra attention to the students. He praised them a lot, checked their homework more carefully, and demanded good work from them. Because of this, the students started doing better. This shows how important expectations are. Therefore, if you want someone to do better, just expect good things from them!

READING COMPREHENSION

1　What is the best title for the passage?

　　a. How to Praise Others
　　b. What You Expect Is What You Get
　　c. Teaching Students with Strict Rules
　　d. The Pygmalion Effect: A Useful Study Skill

2 Which sentence is NOT needed in the passage?

    a. ①   *b.* ②   *c.* ③   *d.* ④

3 What is the best pair for blanks (A) and (B)?

	(A)		(B)
a.	more experience	—	less experience
b.	high intelligence	—	low intelligence
c.	high expectations	—	low expectations
d.	good relationships	—	bad relationships

4 What can be inferred from the underlined part?

    a. The selected students all had the same IQ.

    b. The students were actually smarter than the others.

    c. Researchers didn't care how many students were selected.

    d. Some of the students could have been less smart than the others.

5 Why did the randomly selected students get higher grades than the others?

_____

6 Using the Pygmalion effect, what is a teacher UNLIKELY to do to help students do well?

    a. Tell them that they're doing a good job

    b. Give them easier work

    c. Check what the students do with more attention

    d. Ask them to show more effort

STRATEGIC ORGANIZER

Fill in the blanks with the correct words.

The Pygmalion Effect – Higher expectations make people perform better.

A classroom experiment
- Several students were _____ selected.
- The teacher was told they were _____ than the others.
- They actually did better in class than their classmates.

What caused the results
- The teacher gave more _____ to the selected students.
- _____ more from students helps them succeed.

smarter	attention	carefully	randomly	expecting

VOCABULARY REVIEW

A Complete the sentences with the words in the box. (Change the form if needed.)

surprisingly	praise	badly	effect	genius

1 Albert Einstein was a(n) _____ in physics.

2 Increasing levels of CO_2 cause the greenhouse _____.

3 I was disappointed because I did _____ on my exams.

4 She _____ her workers for their hard work this morning.

B Find the word that has a similar meaning to the underlined word.

1 He was <u>selected</u> for the national soccer team.

    a. raised   *b.* invited   *c.* chosen   *d.* sent

2 According to the weather forecast, it will <u>probably</u> rain tomorrow.

    a. hardly   *b.* likely   *c.* finally   *d.* surely

C Choose the best word to complete each sentence.

1 He was not able to meet his parents' _____ and let them down.

    a. expectations   *b.* mistakes   *c.* faces   *d.* classes

2 He had such good _____ this year that he received a scholarship.

    a. health   *b.* grades   *c.* friends   *d.* excuses

3 I was lucky to stay there one more night at no _____ cost.

    a. far   *b.* less   *c.* extra   *d.* many

4 I don't know what I'm going to do. What would you do in my _____?

    a. mind   *b.* head   *c.* pocket   *d.* situation

Unit ★ 18

TRAVEL

A Connect each word to its correct definition.

1 to move along or through a place · · **a.** pass

2 a part of the face, like the eyes or nose · · **b.** height

3 the distance from the bottom of something to the top · · **c.** feature

4 a place where people go to see animals that live in water · · **d.** aquarium

B Write the word that has a similar meaning to each word.

fear	visitor	view	stunning

1 sight : _____

2 panic : _____

3 guest : _____

4 wonderful : _____

★ Asahiyama Zoo

Before Reading

If you could change zoos to make them more fun, what would you do?

Yesterday, I visited Asahiyama Zoo in Hokkaido. The exhibits are cleverly designed. Visitors can watch animals' behavior and their features from very close up. I loved it!

My favorite part was the penguin aquarium. It has an underwater tunnel with glass walls on all sides. It provides a stunning view. Inside the tunnel, I could see penguins swimming fast above my head. I felt as if they were _____(A)_____!

Seeing the polar bears and seals was great, too. (①) The polar bears made a huge splash when they jumped into the water. (②) The seals passed through them while they swam. (③) I enjoyed watching them from just a few centimeters away. (④)

I also loved watching the orangutans. They have a giant set of ropes to
15 play on that is 17 meters off the ground. Though it looked really dangerous, they climbed and hung from it. In nature, orangutans live in trees. So they can easily move around at such heights without fear.

I heard there is a special event called the Penguin Walk in winter. I want to visit the zoo again to see it!

READING COMPREHENSION

1 What is the passage mainly about?

a. Museum exhibits in Hokkaido
b. Special animals living only in zoos
c. The strange behavior of sea animals
d. A famous tourist attraction in Hokkaido

2 What made the writer think Asahiyama Zoo is special?

    a. Its huge size   *b.* Its beautiful scenery

    c. Its popularity among tourists   *d.* Its creative ways of showing animals

3 What is the best choice for blank (A)?

    a. lying   *b.* flying   *c.* jumping   *d.* walking

4 Where would the following sentence best fit?

> And the seal aquarium has special glass tubes.

    a. ①   *b.* ②   *c.* ③   *d.* ④

5 What kind of event is held in the zoo in winter?

_____

6 Write T if the statement is true or F if it's false.

    1) In the penguin aquarium, people can see penguins on all sides.

    2) Orangutans are afraid of hanging from the ropes.

STRATEGIC ORGANIZER

Fill in the blanks with the correct words.

A Visit to Asahiyama Zoo

Penguin aquarium
- Underwater _____ with a glass view
- Penguins' swimming that looks like flying

Polar bear and seal aquarium
- Polar bears making a big _____ when diving
- Seals swimming through glass _____

Orangutan cage
- A set of ropes at a height of 17 m
- Orangutans showing their _____ moves

> tubes   skillful   tunnel   behavior   splash

★ ★ ★ VOCABULARY REVIEW

A Write the correct word next to its definition.

seal	exhibit	rope	underwater	huge

1 extremely large in size: _____

2 being under the surface of water: _____

3 a collection of things that are publicly displayed: _____

4 a thick cord made by twisting many thinner strings: _____

B Find the word that has the opposite meaning of the underlined word.

1 I will climb the mountain on New Year's Day to see the sunrise.

   a. descend   *b.* rise   *c.* bring   *d.* believe

2 There was a giant table in the center of the room.

   a. real   *b.* tiny   *c.* alive   *d.* clever

C Choose the best word to complete each sentence.

1 I watched every movie that he starred in because he's my _____ actor.

   a. favorite   *b.* different   *c.* economic   *d.* traditional

2 Rachel dove into the pool and made a big _____.

   a. nature   *b.* splash   *c.* type   *d.* jump

3 It suddenly became dark because the train entered a _____.

   a. trap   *b.* highway   *c.* tunnel   *d.* disaster

4 Alex called me and apologized for his rude _____.

   a. benefit   *b.* prison   *c.* exhibition   *d.* behavior

Unit ★ 19
FASHION

A Connect each word to its correct definition.

1 with little or no hair on the head • • *a.* bald

2 people from the family of a king and queen • • *b.* judge

3 something used to represent something else • • *c.* royalty

4 a person who makes decisions in court cases • • *d.* symbol

B Write the word that has a similar meaning to each word.

copy	recent	status	directly

1 rank : _____   *2* imitate : _____

3 current : _____   *4* straight : _____

Today, many people love wearing wigs. However, this isn't just a recent fashion. Wigs have been worn throughout history. Also, they have had different _____(A)_____ depending on time and place.

5   In ancient Egyptian times, people wore wigs for practical reasons — to keep their heads clean and to hide them from the sun. At that time, they shaved off their hair to avoid getting *lice. But that meant the hot desert sun would shine directly onto their bald heads. So they needed wigs to

10 protect their heads.

    From the 16th to the 18th century in Western Europe, wearing wigs was a way to show one's _____(B)_____. Queen Elizabeth I of England and Louis XIII of France wore wigs to improve their appearance, and the upper classes started copying them. Soon, wigs became very popular. ① However, not everyone was allowed to wear wigs. ② Only royalty and high-ranking officials could wear them. ③ High-ranking officials had many servants. ④ Therefore, wearing wigs became a symbol of one's high place in society. Now wigs are no longer worn for this purpose. But judges in British courts still wear white wigs to honor the long tradition.

*lice: small insects that live on people's bodies

READING COMPREHENSION

1 **What is the passage mainly about?**

   a. What styles of wigs people wore in the past
   b. How high class people started wearing wigs
   c. How wigs have been used throughout history
   d. Why wigs became popular in the fashion industry

2 What is the best choice for blank (A)?

   a. roles

   b. styles

   c. colors

   d. materials

3 Why did ancient Egyptians need to protect their heads after shaving off their hair?

_____

4 What is the best choice for blank (B)?

   a. age   *b.* mood

   c. social status   *d.* family tradition

5 Which sentence is NOT needed in the passage?

   a. ①   *b.* ②   *c.* ③   *d.* ④

6 Write T if the statement is true or F if it's false.

   1) People have only recently started wearing wigs.

   2) British judges still wear wigs in court today.

STRATEGIC ORGANIZER

Fill in the blanks with the correct words.

Wigs in Different Times and Places

Ancient Egypt
- People kept their heads free of lice by _____ off their hair.
- They wore wigs to protect their bald heads from the _____.

16th-18th century Europe
- People wore wigs to show high social _____.
- Queens and kings wore wigs and influenced the _____ classes.

sun   status   royalty   upper   shaving

★ ★ ★ VOCABULARY REVIEW

A Write the correct word next to its definition.

| court | official | honor | social | shave |

1 to cut off body hair from the skin: _____

2 connected to society or people's lives: _____

3 to show respect for someone or something: _____

4 a place where a judge decides whether someone is guilty or not: _____

B Find the word that has the opposite meaning of the underlined word.

1 Children under 15 years old are not <u>allowed</u> to see this movie.

   a. assisted   *b.* released   *c.* prohibited   *d.* encouraged

2 The linguist found out that this language was used in <u>ancient</u> Rome.

   a. popular   *b.* modern   *c.* common   *d.* old-fashioned

C Choose the best word to complete each sentence.

1 I tried to keep warm to _____ catching a cold.

   a. avoid   *b.* provide   *c.* suggest   *d.* consider

2 This handy umbrella is _____ during the rainy season.

   a. upper   *b.* strict   *c.* practical   *d.* high-ranking

3 The sun was _____ through the window, so I drew a curtain.

   a. hanging   *b.* shining   *c.* clearing   *d.* expressing

4 If you want to _____ your eyes from the sun, wear dark sunglasses.

   a. ignore   *b.* escape   *c.* protect   *d.* describe

Unit ★ 20
ISSUES

★ ──── VOCABULARY PREVIEW ──── ★

A Connect each word to its correct definition.

1 perfectly correct • • **a.** suffer

2 to experience physical or mental pain • • **b.** terrible

3 causing or involving serious harm or injury • • **c.** accurate

4 something that sick people take to get healthy • • **d.** medicine

B Write the word that has the opposite meaning of each word.

pain	stressed	safety	useful

1 danger : _____   2 relaxed : _____

3 comfort : _____   4 impractical : _____

★ *Animal Testing*

Scientists sometimes use animals to test the safety of new medicines. Some people think this is necessary, but others think it should be banned.

Jason: I think saving human lives is the most
5 important thing. Medicine must be tested before it is used on people. For a long time, animal testing has been the best way to find out if medicine is safe. Without using animals in their experiments, scientists wouldn't be able to find cures for terrible diseases.

10 **Amy:** Animals can feel pain just like people! Many animals suffer and die in the experiments. We have no right to be cruel to animals. Scientists need to find a way of testing new medicines that doesn't hurt animals. An animal's life is just as important as a person's.

15 **Patrick:** Animal testing is useful not only for humans but also for animals. Scientists have invented many kinds of medicine that help animals stay healthy. But this wouldn't have been possible without animal testing.

Sue: Does animal testing really work? Scientists
20 might find that a new kind of medicine doesn't harm mice. But that doesn't necessarily mean that it won't harm humans! _____(A)_____, according to some reports, test animals get so stressed that the results aren't always accurate.

READING COMPREHENSION

1 **What is the best title for the passage?**

- *a.* How Does Animal Testing Work?
- *b.* Should We Allow Animal Testing?
- *c.* Why Do We Need to Protect Animals?
- *d.* What Are the Problems of Animal Testing?

2 Jason thinks animal testing is necessary because _____.

    a. it helps save sick animals

    b. the test results are always accurate

    c. it costs less than other testing methods

    d. it makes sure that medicines are safe to take

3 In Patrick's opinion, how has animal testing benefited animal health?

Through animal testing, _____.

4 What is the best choice for blank (A)?

    a. Instead   *b.* Therefore   *c.* However   *d.* Furthermore

5 What does Sue think about animal testing?

    a. It has helped save human lives.

    b. We can't always trust its results.

    c. It seriously hurts the test animals.

    d. There is a safer way to protect animals.

6 Who has the same opinion as that expressed in the following statement?

We don't have the right to make animals suffer for us.

    a. Jason   *b.* Amy   *c.* Patrick   *d.* Sue

STRATEGIC ORGANIZER

Fill in the blanks with the correct words.

Animal Testing

Jason
- 1) _____ are most important.
- Animal testing helps find cures for deadly diseases.

Amy
- Animals are as important as people.
- Animal testing causes them to feel 2) _____.

Patrick
- It doesn't only help humans.
- It finds cures for 3) _____ diseases, too.

Sue
- It may not prove that medicine is 4) _____.
- Results are not always accurate.

safe   pain   humans   animal   mice

★ ★ ★
VOCABULARY REVIEW

A Complete the sentences with the words in the box. (Change the form if needed.)

right	invent	cure	report	hurt

1 If we find a(n) _____ for this illness, we can save a lot of lives.

2 You have no _____ to complain. It's you who made the mistake.

3 He has _____ a complex device that removes salt from seawater.

4 A recent _____ shows that about 40 percent of the population supports the new law.

B Find the word that has the opposite meaning of the underlined word.

1 The king was so cruel that all the people hated him.

   a. kind   b. weak   c. strict   d. wild

2 Riding bikes on the street is banned in some cities.

   a. protected   b. allowed   c. avoided   d. forbidden

C Choose the best word to complete each sentence.

1 They carried out a(n) _____ to test a new theory.

   a. popularity b. result   c. weight   d. experiment

2 I hope that when I get old, my mind will _____ young.

   a. die   b. stay   c. taste   d. leave

3 Just because he is smart, that doesn't _____ mean he is a good student.

   a. necessarily b. hardly   c. never   d. carefully

4 The pills didn't _____ for me, so I'm taking different ones.

   a. react   b. destroy   c. test   d. work

Reading FORWARD

BASIC 2

★ Word Book ★

Unit ★ 01 JOBS

tester	명 검사자
test	동 실험하다, 테스트하다
product	명 제품
properly	부 제대로
closely	부 면밀히
figure out	…을 알아내다
cause	명 원인
problem	명 문제
fix	동 (문제 등을) 바로잡다
release	동 공개하다, 발표하다
afterwards	부 나중에
correct	동 수정하다
various	형 다양한
suggest	동 제안하다
try out	…을 시험적으로 사용해보다
basically	부 기본적으로
knowledge	명 지식
communicator	명 의사를 전달하는 사람
patience	명 인내력
require	동 필요로 하다
compare	동 비교하다
contrast	동 대조하다

general	⟨형⟩ 일반적인, 보편적인
bug	⟨명⟩ 벌레; (프로그램 등의) 오류
technical	⟨형⟩ 기술적인; 전문적인
define	⟨동⟩ 정의하다
over and over	여러 번 되풀이하여

Unit ★ 02 CULTURE

normally	⟨부⟩ 보통
funeral	⟨명⟩ 장례식
serious	⟨형⟩ 진지한
dress	⟨동⟩ 옷을 입다
wail	⟨동⟩ 통곡하다, 흐느끼다
develop	⟨동⟩ 발달시키다
tradition	⟨명⟩ 전통
body	⟨명⟩ 몸; 시체
cemetery	⟨명⟩ 묘지
dead	⟨형⟩ 죽은
brass	⟨명⟩ 황동; 금관악기
band	⟨명⟩ (금관악기 등을 연주하는) 악단
march	⟨동⟩ 행진하다 ⟨명⟩ 행진
cheerful	⟨형⟩ 발랄한, 유쾌한
beat	⟨명⟩ 리듬

wild	형 야생의; 격렬한
origin	명 기원
period	명 기간
slavery	명 노예 (상태 · 신분); 노예제도
slave	명 노예
release	동 풀어주다, 해방하다
celebrate	동 기념하다, 축하하다
popularity	명 인기
usual	형 보통의, 평상시의
include	동 포함하다
consider	동 여기다

Unit ★ 03 TEENS

speech	명 연설
whole	형 전체의
nervous	형 불안해 하는
nervousness	명 불안, 초조
in public	사람들이 있는 데서
shake	동 흔들리다
bright	형 (색깔이) 선명한, 밝은
beat	동 이기다; (심장이) 고동치다
rapidly	부 빨리, 급속히

fear	몡 두려움
public	혱 대중의; 공개적인
overcome	동 극복하다
tip	몡 조언
normal	혱 정상적인
release	동 방출하다
hormone	몡 호르몬
accept	동 받아들이다
make use of	…을 이용하다
audience	몡 청중, 관중
interested	혱 흥미 있어 하는
prepare	동 준비하다
carefully	뷰 조심스럽게; 정성을 들여
familiar	혱 친숙한
performance	몡 수행, 실행
perform	동 수행하다, 실행하다
advantage	몡 장점
deliver	동 배달하다; (연설·강연 등을) 하다
control	동 통제하다
lively	혱 생기 넘치는
treat	동 대하다, 다루다
serve	동 제공하다
practice	몡 연습

pet	몡 애완동물
blood	몡 혈액
human	몡 인간, 사람
donation	몡 기부, 기증
donate	동 기부하다, 기증하다
sick	혱 아픈, 병든
collect	동 모으다
save	동 (죽음 등에서) 구하다
life	몡 생명
owner	몡 주인
donor	몡 기증자
weigh	동 무게가 …이다
up to date	최신의
result	몡 결과
delicious	혱 아주 맛있는
in need	어려움에 처한
benefit	몡 혜택, 이득

heaven	몡 천국
desert	몡 사막
locate	동 …에 두다[놓다]
unearthly	혱 기이한
landscape	몡 풍경
situate	동 위치시키다
height	몡 높이
shine	동 빛나다, 반짝이다
endless	혱 끝없는
scenery	몡 경치
appear	동 나타나다
disappear	동 사라지다
giant	혱 거대한
thin	혱 얇은
layer	몡 막, 층
reflect	동 비추다
highland	몡 산악 지대
billion	몡 10억
death	몡 죽음
take up	(시간 · 공간을) 차지하다
amazed	혱 놀란
confused	혱 혼란스러운

| disappointed | 형 실망한 |

Unit★06 LITERATURE

excellent	형 훌륭한
detective	명 탐정
professor	명 교수
college	명 대학
happen	동 (일 · 사건 등이) 일어나다
scholarship	명 장학금
copy	명 복사본; (책 · 신문 등의) 한 부 동 베끼다, 복사하다
appointment	명 약속
return	동 돌아오다
servant	명 하인
by mistake	실수로
notice	동 알아차리다
scratch	명 긁힌 자국
guess	동 추측하다
in a hurry	급히
question	동 질문하다, 심문하다
incident	명 일, 사건
damage	동 피해를 입히다

reputation	몡 평판, 명성
in secret	비밀리에
case	몡 경우; 사건
mysterious	혱 불가사의한, 비밀스러운
note	몡 메모
suspect	동 의심하다

Unit ★ *07* SPORTS

wonder	동 궁금해하다
refer to	…을 나타내다
possession	몡 소유; (공을) 차지한 상태
possess	동 소유하다, 점유하다
amount	몡 양
automatic	혱 자동의
analysis	몡 분석
analyze	동 분석하다
device	몡 장치
place	동 설치하다, 놓다
record	동 녹화하다, 기록하다
recording	몡 녹음, 녹화(된 것)
field	몡 경기장
dot	몡 점

count	⑧ 계산하다
divide	⑧ 분할하다; (…을) …으로 나누다
support	⑲ 지원, 도움
care about	…에 관심을 가지다
guarantee	⑧ 보장하다
victory	⑲ 승리
opposing	⑱ (팀·군대 등이) 서로 겨루는
key	⑱ 중요한, 핵심적인
advanced	⑱ 선진의
purpose	⑲ 용도, 목적
measure	⑧ 측정하다
monitor	⑧ 감시하다
assist	⑧ 돕다

Unit ★ *08* PEOPLE

well-known	⑱ 유명한
musician	⑲ 음악가
stage	⑲ 무대
blind	⑱ 눈이 먼
blindness	⑲ 실명
shortly	⑭ 곧
birth	⑲ 출생

discourage	동 막다, 단념시키다
overcome	동 극복하다
naturally	부 자연스럽게
master	동 …을 완전히 익히다
various	형 여러 가지의
instrument	명 기구; 악기
recognize	동 알아보다
talent	명 재능
hit	명 타격; 히트 곡[음반]
award	명 상
surgery	명 수술
unfortunately	부 불행하게도
character	명 성격, 성질
inner	형 내부의
positive	형 긍정적인
disability	명 장애
loving	형 다정한
pain	명 고통
perform	동 공연하다

Unit ★ 09 FOOD

| produce | 동 생산하다 |

worldwide	부 전 세계에
bring	동 가져오다, 데려오다
harmful	형 해로운
rumor	명 소문
poisonous	형 독이 있는
substance	명 물질
acid	명 산, 산성
legend	명 전설
name	동 이름을 지어주다
prove	동 증명하다
crowd	명 군중
expect	동 예상[기대]하다
ill	형 아픈, 병든
prevent	동 막다, 예방하다
disease	명 질병
blood pressure	혈압
cancer	명 암
rich	형 부유한; …이 풍부한
include	동 포함하다
introduce	동 소개하다; 들여오다
misunderstood	형 오해를 받는
confuse	동 혼란시키다
maintain	동 유지하다
stomach	명 위
digest	동 소화시키다

Unit ★ 10 ECONOMY

hand	통 건네다
latest	형 최신의
work	통 일하다; 작동되다
advertise	통 광고하다
undercover	형 비밀의, 비밀리에 하는
friendly	형 친절한, 우호적인
consumer	명 소비자
hang out	(…에서) 시간을 보내다
force	통 강요하다
aim	명 목표
effective	형 효과적인
regular	형 규칙적인; 일반적인, 보통의
commercial	명 광고
trust	통 신뢰하다
review	명 논평, 비평
recommend	통 추천하다
recommendation	명 추천
recognize	통 알아보다, 인지하다
unique	형 독특한
invent	통 발명하다
method	명 방법
word-of-mouth	형 구전의, 구두의

critical	형 비판적인

Unit ★ 11 FESTIVALS

celebrate	동 기념하다, 축하하다
wish	명 소원
luck	명 행운; 운
festival	명 축제
festive	형 축제의, 축하하는
temple	명 사원, 절
clear	동 치우다; 맑게 하다
throw	동 던지다
stranger	명 낯선 사람
bucket	명 양동이
refreshing	형 신선한, 상쾌하게 하는
symbolize	동 상징하다
wash off	씻어내다
misfortune	명 불운
traditionally	부 전통적으로
politely	부 정중히
pour	동 붓다
bowl	명 그릇
mood	명 분위기

playful	혱 장난기 많은
curious	혱 궁금한, 호기심이 많은
respect	통 존중하다, 존경하다
totally	훈 완전히
wet	혱 젖은
last	통 지속되다
a variety of	다양한

Unit★12 PSYCHOLOGY

cause	통 야기하다, 초래하다
overeat	통 과식하다
hungry	혱 배고픈
hunger	명 배고픔
research	명 연구, 조사
visual	혱 시각의
vision	명 시력, 시각
sign	명 신호, 표시
have an effect on	…에 영향을 미치다
determine	통 결심하다; 결정하다
bowl	명 그릇
hidden	혱 숨겨진
tube	명 관

bottom	⑲ 바닥, 맨 아래
decrease	⑧ 줄다, 감소하다
stomach	⑲ 위
affect	⑧ 영향을 미치다
be on a diet	다이어트 중이다
secretly	⑨ 몰래
add	⑧ 더하다

Unit ⋆ 13 SCIENCE

object	⑲ 물체
satellite	⑲ 인공위성
send	⑧ 보내다
space	⑲ 우주
launch	⑧ 발사하다
shape	⑧ …의 모양으로 만들다
weigh	⑧ 무게가 …이다
atmosphere	⑲ 대기
technology	⑲ (과학) 기술
improve	⑧ 개선되다
belong to	… 소유이다, …에 속하다
military	⑲ 군대
track	⑧ 추적하다

location	몡 위치
direction	몡 방향; (pl.) 지시, 명령
possible	휑 가능한
impossible	휑 불가능한
predict	동 예측하다
signal	몡 신호
bounce	동 (소리 · 빛이) 반사하다
modern	휑 현대의
artificial	휑 인공의
sector	몡 부문, 분야

Unit ★ 14 SOCIETY

talent	몡 재능
skill	몡 기량; 기술
term	몡 용어
public	휑 공공의
good	몡 선(善); 이익
normally	투 보통
charge	동 (요금 · 값을) 청구하다
legal	휑 법률과 관련된
lawyer	몡 변호사
realize	동 깨닫다

professional	몡 전문직 종사자 혱 전문적인
organize	통 조직하다
employee	몡 고용인
set up	설치하다
involve	통 수반하다; 참여시키다
joy	몡 즐거움
volunteer work	자원봉사
offer	통 제공하다
spread	몡 확산, 전파
for free	무료로

Unit ★ 15 ENTERTAINMENT

musical	몡 뮤지컬
attract	통 끌어모으다
million	몡 100만
award	몡 상
be based on	…에 바탕을 두다
screenplay	몡 영화 대본
lyric	몡 (pl.) 가사
boxer	몡 권투 선수
realize	통 깨닫다
achieve	통 성취하다

awesome	형 굉장한, 엄청난
move	동 움직이다; 감동시키다
passion	명 열정
electricity	명 전기
spark	명 불꽃
cinema	명 영화관
illegally	부 불법적으로
running time	상영 시간
upset	형 속상한
childhood	명 어린 시절

Unit ★ 16 HUMAN BODY

exercise	명 운동 동 운동하다
painful	형 고통스러운
create	동 창조하다, 만들어내다
active	형 활동적인; 활성의
physically	부 육체적으로
mentally	부 정신적으로
experience	명 경험 동 경험하다
relaxed	형 느긋한, 편안한
tough	형 힘든
athlete	명 운동선수

injure	동 부상을 입히다
muscle	명 근육
depressed	형 우울한
regular	형 규칙적인
reward	명 보상
occur	동 일어나다
addicted	형 중독된

Unit ★ 17 EDUCATION

imagine	동 상상하다
smart	형 똑똑한
badly	부 나쁘게
genius	명 천재
remember	동 기억하다
lesson	명 수업; 가르침(의 내용)
situation	명 상황
what is called	소위, 이른바
perform	동 수행하다
poorly	부 좋지 못하게
experiment	명 실험
beginning	명 시작, 초반
researcher	명 연구원

randomly	閉 무작위로
select	图 선발하다
surprisingly	閉 놀랍게도
expect	图 기대하다
expectation	圆 기대
extra	園 추가의
attention	圆 관심, 주의
praise	图 칭찬하다
demand	图 요구하다
strict	園 엄격한
intelligence	圆 지능
relationship	圆 관계

Unit ★ 18 TRAVEL

exhibit	圆 전시품; 전시회[관]
cleverly	閉 교묘하게, 솜씨 좋게
design	图 설계하다
visitor	圆 방문객, 손님
behavior	圆 행동
feature	圆 특징; 생김새
aquarium	圆 수족관
underwater	園 수중의

stunning	형 아주 멋진
view	명 견해; 광경
polar bear	북극곰
seal	명 바다표범
huge	형 거대한
splash	명 첨벙하는 소리; (물을) 튀김
pass	동 지나가다, 통과하다
giant	형 거대한
rope	명 끈, 줄
hang	동 매달리다
height	명 높이
fear	명 두려움
tourist attraction	관광 명소
scenery	명 경치, 풍경
tube	명 관, 통

Unit ★ 19 FASHION

wig	명 가발
recent	형 최근의
throughout	전 … 동안, … 내내
practical	형 실용적인
hide	동 숨다; 가리다, 감추다

shave	동 면도하다
avoid	동 막다, 방지하다
desert	명 사막
directly	부 곧장
bald	형 대머리의
protect	동 보호하다
upper	형 위쪽의
class	명 계급
copy	동 복사하다; 모방하다, 따라 하다
royalty	명 왕족
high-ranking	형 고위의
official	명 관리
symbol	명 상징
judge	명 판사
court	명 법정
honor	동 존중하다
industry	명 산업
material	명 재료
status	명 신분, 지위

Unit ★ 20 ISSUES

safety	몡 안전(성)
medicine	몡 약
ban	동 금지하다
cure	몡 치료법
terrible	혱 끔찍한, 심한
disease	몡 질병
pain	몡 통증, 고통
suffer	동 고통받다
right	몡 권리
cruel	혱 잔혹한
useful	혱 유용한
report	몡 보고서
stressed	혱 스트레스를 받는
accurate	혱 정확한
method	몡 방법

MEMO

Reading FORWARD

BASIC 2

★ Answer Key ★

Reading FORWARD

BASIC 2

★ Answer Key ★

VOCABULARY PREVIEW
A 1 b **2** c **3** a **4** d   **B 1** various **2** cause **3** fix **4** problem

An Interview with a Game Tester

1 b **2** d **3** b **4** a **5** Because he saw Robert's[his] talent for computer games. **6** d

---

이것은 Robert Watson 씨와의 인터뷰입니다. 그는 로스앤젤레스의 유명 컴퓨터 게임 회사의 게임 테스터입니다.

Q: 게임 테스터는 무슨 일을 하나요?

A: 회사들이 신제품들을 판매하기 전에 테스트를 하듯이, 우리도 새로운 게임들이 제대로 작동하는지 확인하기 위해 그것들을 테스트합니다. 우리는 많은 다양한 방식으로 게임을 함으로써 각 게임을 면밀히 확인합니다. 오류나 실수를 발견하면, 우리는 그것들을 게임 프로그래머와 디자이너에게 보고합니다. 그리고 우리는 그들이 원인을 파악하도록 도와주기도 합니다. 모든 문제들이 해결되면, 회사는 그 게임을 출시할 수 있습니다. 심지어 그 후에도, 우리는 사용자들에 의해 발견된 다른 오류들을 수정해야 합니다.

Q: 왜 당신은 이 직업을 선택하셨나요?

A: 저의 형은 게임 디자이너입니다. 제가 다양한 종류의 게임을 하는 것을 좋아해서, 그는 종종 제게 자신이 만든 게임을 살펴봐 달라고 부탁했습니다. 그가 컴퓨터 게임에 대한 제 재능을 보았기 때문에, 그는 제게 게임 테스터가 되라고 제안했습니다. 게다가, 새로운 게임들을 처음으로 해보는 사람이 되는 것은 신이 났습니다. 그래서 저는 게임 테스터가 되기로 결심했습니다!

Q: 게임 테스터들은 어떤 역량이 필요한가요?

A: 기본적으로 게임 테스터들에게는 컴퓨터 시스템에 대한 지식이 필요합니다. 이에 더하여, 그들은 게임 디자이너들에게 문제점을 명확히 설명할 수 있는 훌륭한 의사 전달자여야 합니다. 가장 중요하게는, 똑같은 게임을 계속해서 테스트하기 때문에 인내심이 요구됩니다.

어휘   tester[téstər] 명 검사자 (test 동 실험하다, 테스트하다)   product[prádʌkt] 명 제품
properly[prápərli] 부 제대로   closely[klóusli] 부 면밀히   figure out …을 알아내다
cause[kɔːz] 명 원인   problem[prábləm] 명 문제   fix[fiks] 동 (문제 등을) 바로잡다
release[rilíːs] 동 공개하다, 발표하다   afterwards[æftərwərdz] 부 나중에
correct[kərékt] 동 수정하다   various[véəriəs] 형 다양한   suggest[səgdʒést] 동 제안하다
try out …을 시험적으로 사용해보다   basically[béisikəli] 부 기본적으로
knowledge[nálidʒ] 명 지식   communicator[kəmjúːnəkèitər] 명 의사를 전달하는 사람
patience[péiʃəns] 명 인내력   require[rikwáiər] 동 필요로 하다   [문제] compare[kəmpéər]
동 비교하다   contrast[kəntrǽst] 동 대조하다   general[dʒénərəl] 형 일반적인, 보편적인
bug[bʌg] 명 벌레; *(프로그램 등의) 오류   technical[téknikəl] 형 기술적인; 전문적인
define[difáin] 동 정의하다   over and over 여러 번 되풀이하여

구문   6행   …, we test new games **to see** [*if* they work properly].
• to see: '…하기 위해'라는 의미로, 목적을 나타내는 부사적 용법의 to부정사
• if: '…인지 (아닌지)'의 의미로, 동사 see의 목적어인 명사절을 이끄는 접속사

10행   Even afterwards, we need to correct other errors [**found** by users].
• found 이하는 other errors를 수식하는 과거분사구

12행   …, so he often **asked** me **to check** the games [(which[that]) *he made*].
• ask + 목적어 + to-v: …에게 ~할 것을 요청하다

- he made 앞에 the games를 선행사로 하는 목적격 관계대명사가 생략되어 있음

14행 ..., he **suggested** that I (should) **become** a game tester.
- 제안을 나타내는 동사 suggest 뒤에 이어지는 that절의 동사는 'should + 동사원형'을 쓰는데, should는 종종 생략됨

14행 Besides, **it** was exciting **to be** the first person *to try out* new games.
- it은 가주어이고, to be 이하가 진주어
- to try out: the first person을 수식하는 형용사적 용법의 to부정사

STRATEGIC SUMMARY   problems, interested, skills, patience

VOCABULARY REVIEW

A   *1* talent   *2* reported   *3* try out   *4* decided
B   *1* d   *2* c   C   *1* a   *2* b   *3* d   *4* c

★unit★ 02 CULTURE

pp. 13-16

VOCABULARY PREVIEW

A   *1* a   *2* d   *3* c   *4* b   B   *1* wild   *2* dead   *3* cheerful   *4* dress

★Jazz Funerals

1 c   *2* b   *3* b   *4* b   *5* Because they lived hard lives and thought death could release them from slavery.   *6* c

> 보통, 장례식은 슬프고 진지하다. 검은 옷을 입은 사람들은 종종 울고 통곡한다. 그러나 New Orleans의 흑인들은 다른 전통을 발달시켰다. 그들은 때때로 '재즈 장례식'을 치른다.
> 재즈 장례식은 처음에는 보통의 장례식처럼 보인다. 차 한 대가 시신을 묘지로 데려갈 때, 고인의 가족과 친구들이 조용히 따라간다. 관악대도 슬픈 곡을 연주하며 그들과 함께 행진한다. 그러나 그들이 묘지에서 돌아올 때 모든 것이 바뀐다. 악단은 발랄한 곡을 연주하기 시작하고, 리듬은 더 빨라지고 더 격렬해진다. 길거리의 사람들이 종종 음악에 맞춰 노래하고 춤추기 위해 그 행진에 동참한다.
> 재즈 장례식의 기원은 아직 노예제가 있던 시기인 18세기로 거슬러 올라간다. 노예들은 힘든 삶을 살았고, 죽음이 그들을 노예 신분으로부터 해방해 줄 수 있다고 생각했다. 그래서 그들은 노래하고 춤을 춤으로써 고인의 자유를 축하했다. 그들은 또한 노래와 춤이 고인으로 하여금 천국으로 가는 길을 찾는 데 도움을 준다고 생각했다. 20세기에, 사람들은 장례식에서 재즈를 연주하기 시작했다. 이러한 장례식이 '재즈 장례식'이라고 알려지게 되었다.
> 재즈 장례식에서 사람들은 흥겨워하지만, 사람들이 다른 모든 장례식에서 그러하듯이 그들은 여전히 고인에 대한 사랑을 표현한다.

어휘   normally[nɔ́:rməli] 🄫 보통   funeral[fjú:nərəl] 🄫 장례식   serious[síəriəs] 🄫 진지한
dress[dres] 🄫 옷을 입다   wail[weil] 🄫 통곡하다, 흐느끼다   develop[divéləp] 🄫 발달시키다
tradition[trədíʃən] 🄫 전통   body[bάdi] 🄫 몸; *시체   cemetery[sémətèri] 🄫 묘지
dead[ded] 🄫 죽은   brass[bræs] 🄫 황동; *금관악기   band[bænd] 🄫 (금관악기 등을 연주하는) 악단
march[ma:rtʃ] 🄫 행진하다 🄫 행진   cheerful[tʃíərfəl] 🄫 발랄한, 유쾌한   beat[bi:t] 🄫 리듬
wild[waild] 🄫 야생의; *격렬한   origin[ɔ́:rədʒin] 🄫 기원   period[píːəriəd] 🄫 기간
slavery[sléivəri] 🄫 노예 (상태·신분); 노예제도 (slave 🄫 노예)   release[rilí:s] 🄫 풀어주다, 해방하다
celebrate[séləbrèit] 🄫 기념하다, 축하하다   [문제] popularity[pὰpjulǽrəti] 🄫 인기
usual[júːʒuəl] 🄫 보통의, 평상시의   include[inklúːd] 🄫 포함하다   consider[kənsídər] 🄫 여기다

1행 People [**dressed** in black] often cry and wail.
- dressed 이하는 People을 수식하는 과거분사구

4행 **As** a car takes the body to the cemetery, family and friends of *the dead* follow quietly.
- as: '…할 때'라는 의미의 접속사
- the + 형용사: '…하는 사람들'이라는 의미로, 복수 보통 명사로 쓰임

5행 A brass band also marches with them, **playing** sad music.
- playing 이하는 동시동작을 나타내는 분사구문

9행 The origin of jazz funerals goes back to the 18th century, a period [**when** there was still slavery].
- when 이하는 a period를 수식하는 관계부사절

14행 They also thought (that) **singing** and **dancing** *helped* the dead *find* their way to heaven.
- singing과 dancing은 각각 that절의 주어로 쓰인 동명사
- help + 목적어 + 동사원형: …가 ~하도록 돕다

STRATEGIC ORGANIZER   normal, joyful, free, heaven

VOCABULARY REVIEW

A   **1** march   **2** funeral   **3** serious   **4** usual
B   **1** c   **2** d   **C**   **1** d   **2** a   **3** b   **4** c

03 TEENS

pp. 17-20

VOCABULARY PREVIEW

A   **1** d   **2** c   **3** b   **4** a   **B**   **1** accept   **2** bright   **3** interested   **4** public

★Terry's Problem

1 d   **2** Because they don't want to make mistakes in front of other people.   **3** c   **4** c   **5** b   **6** b

---

Page 박사님께,

저는 다음 주에 저희 학급 전체 앞에서 연설해야 해요. 저는 그것 때문에 정말 초조해요. 사람들 앞에서 말을 할 때마다, 제 손은 떨리고, 제 얼굴은 선홍색이 되며, 제 심장은 빠르게 뜁니다. 제가 어떻게 해야 할까요?

Terry

Terry에게,

당신은 사람들 앞에서 말하는 것에 대한 두려움이 있는지도 모릅니다. 이것은 아주 흔한데, 왜냐하면 아무도 다른 사람들 앞에서 실수하고 싶어 하지 않기 때문입니다. 당신은 이러한 조언들을 따름으로써 이 두려움을 극복할 수 있습니다.

첫째, 초조해지는 것이 정상이라는 점을 기억하세요. 사실, 약간의 두려움은 당신에게 도움이 될 수 있습니다! 당신이 초조해질 때, 당신의 몸은 아드레날린이라고 불리는 호르몬을 분비합니다. 이는 당신을 생기 넘치게 하고 당신이 더 잘하도록 도움을 주는 더 많은 에너지를 당신에게 줍니다. 그러니 당신의 초조함을 받아들이고 그것을 잘 활용하려고 노력하세요.

다음으로, 청중들을 겁내지 않도록 노력하세요. 그들을 당신의 친구들이라고 생각하세요. 이야기할 때, 미소를 짓고 청중들의 눈을 바라보세요. 이렇게 하면, 그들은 더 흥미를 느낄 것입니다. 그리고 그것은 연설하는 것을 더 쉽게 만들어줍니다.

어휘 speech[spi:tʃ] 몡 연설   whole[houl] 혱 전체의   nervous[nə́:rvəs] 혱 불안해 하는
(nervousness 몡 불안, 초조)   in public 사람들이 있는 데서   shake[ʃeik] 동 흔들리다
bright[brait] 혱 (색깔이) 선명한, 밝은   beat[bi:t] 동 이기다; *(심장이) 고동치다   rapidly[rǽpidli] 뷔
빨리, 급속히   fear[fiər] 몡 두려움   public[pʌ́blik] 혱 대중의; *공개적인   overcome[òuvərkʌ́m]
동 극복하다   tip[tip] 몡 조언   normal[nɔ́:rməl] 혱 정상적인   release[rilí:s] 동 방출하다
hormone[hɔ́:rmòun] 몡 호르몬   accept[æksépt] 동 받아들이다   make use of …을 이용하다
audience[ɔ́:diəns] 몡 청중, 관중   interested[íntərəstid] 혱 흥미 있어 하는   prepare[pripéər]
동 준비하다   carefully[kɛ́ərfəli] 뷔 조심스럽게; *정성을 들여   familiar[fəmíljər] 혱 친숙한
performance[pərfɔ́:rməns] 몡 수행, 실행 (perform 동 수행하다, 실행하다)
[문제] advantage[ædvǽntidʒ] 몡 장점   deliver[dilívər] 동 배달하다; *(연설 · 강연 등을) 하다
control[kəntróul] 동 통제하다   lively[láivli] 혱 생기 넘치는   treat[tri:t] 동 대하다, 다루다
serve[sə:rv] 동 제공하다   practice[prǽktis] 몡 연습

구문 4행 **Every time** I speak in public, my hands shake, ….
• every time …: …할 때마다

13행 When you become nervous, your body releases a hormone [**called** adrenaline].
• called 이하는 a hormone을 수식하는 과거분사구

16행 Next, **try** *not* **to be** afraid of the audience.
• try to-v: …하려고 애쓰다
• not to-v: to부정사의 부정은 to부정사 앞에 not을 붙임

18행 And that **makes** giving the speech **easier**.
• make + 목적어 + 형용사: …을 ~하게 하다

21행 **The more familiar** you are with the speech, **the better** your performance will be.
• the + 비교급 …, the + 비교급 ~: …하면 할수록 더 ~하다

STRATEGIC ORGANIZER mistakes, normal, audience, practice

VOCABULARY REVIEW

A **1** whole **2** overcame **3** audience **4** in public
B **1** a **2** d   C **1** b **2** a **3** b **4** d

ANIMALS   pp. 21-24

VOCABULARY PREVIEW

A **1** b **2** a **3** d **4** c   B **1** sick **2** delicious **3** donor **4** collect

★The Pet Blood Bank

1 d **2** It collects other dogs' blood and gives it to them. **3** c **4** b **5** d **6** c

영국에 있는 애완동물 혈액은행에 대해 들어본 적이 있습니까? 사람들처럼 개들도 다칠 수 있고 헌혈이 필요할 수 있습니다. 전국의 아픈 개들을 돕기 위해서, 그곳은 다른 개들의 혈액을 모아서 그들에게 줍니다. 2007년에 이 프로그램이 시작된 이래, 그것은 수천 마리 개들의 생명을 구했습니다!

　　많은 애완동물 주인들이 그들의 개들이 헌혈하게 하기 위해 기꺼이 그들을 데리고 옵니다. 그러나 모든 개가 헌혈할 수 있는 것은 아닙니다. 헌혈할 개는 먼저 건강 검진을 받아야 합니다. (개 주인들은 적어도 일 년에 한 번은 자신의 애완동물을 의사에게 데려가야 합니다.) 헌혈할 개들은 체중이 25kg이 넘어야 하고 한 살에서 여덟 살 사이여야 합니다. 그들은 또한 최신 예방 접종을 모두 해야 합니다. 헌혈할 개가 충분히 건강하다면, 최대 450ml의 혈액을 뽑습니다. 이 혈액량은 다른 개 네 마리의 생명을 구할 수 있습니다!

　　헌혈은 아픈 개들뿐만 아니라 애완동물 주인들 또한 도와줍니다. 건강 검진의 결과는 그들에게 자신의 개의 건강의 중요한 변화들을 보여줄 수 있습니다. 그리고 헌혈한 개들은 헌혈을 한 대가로 맛있는 음료와 비스킷을 받습니다!

어휘　　pet[pet] 명 애완동물　　blood[blʌd] 명 혈액　　human[hjúːmən] 명 인간, 사람
donation[dounéiʃən] 명 기부, 기증 (donate 동 기부하다, 기증하다)　　sick[sik] 형 아픈, 병든
collect[kəlékt] 동 모으다　　save[seiv] 동 (죽음 등에서) 구하다　　life[laif] 명 생명　　owner[óunər]
명 주인　　donor[dóunər] 명 기증자　　weigh[wei] 동 무게가 …이다　　up to date 최신의
result[rizʌ́lt] 명 결과　　delicious[dilíʃəs] 형 아주 맛있는　　[문제] in need 어려움에 처한
benefit[bénəfit] 명 혜택, 이득

구문

1행　　**Have** you **heard** of Pet Blood Bank in the UK?
　　• Have heard: '…한 적이 있다'의 의미로, 경험을 나타내는 현재완료

2행　　**To help** sick dogs across the country, it collects other dogs' blood ….
　　• To help: '…하기 위해'라는 의미로, 목적을 나타내는 부사적 용법의 to부정사

3행　　**Since** this program started in 2007, it *has saved* the lives of thousands of dogs!
　　• since: '…이후[부터] (지금까지)'라는 의미로, 주로 현재완료와 함께 쓰임
　　• has saved: '…해 왔다'의 의미로, 계속을 나타내는 현재완료

5행　　Many pet owners gladly bring their dogs to **have** them **donate** their blood.
　　• 사역동사(have) + 목적어 + 동사원형: …가 ~하게 하다

10행　　If a donor dog is healthy enough, up to 450 ml of blood **will be taken**.
　　• will be taken은 '…이 취해질 것이다'라는 의미로, 조동사와 함께 쓰인 수동태

12행　　[**Donating** blood] helps *not only* sick dogs *but also* pet owners.
　　• Donating 이하는 문장의 주어 역할을 하는 동명사구
　　• not only A but also B: A뿐만 아니라 B도

STRATEGIC SUMMARY　　donor, save, health, delicious

VOCABULARY REVIEW

A　　**1** blood　　**2** donation　　**3** enough　　**4** owner
B　　**1** d　　**2** d　　　C　　**1** a　　**2** b　　**3** b　　**4** d

05 PLACES

pp. 25-28

VOCABULARY PREVIEW

A　　**1** d　　**2** c　　**3** a　　**4** b　　　B　　**1** heaven　　**2** giant　　**3** thin　　**4** endless

★*The Salar de Uyuni*

1 b　**2** b　**3** c　**4** b　**5** c　**6** The dry air of the Bolivian highlands caused all of the water to disappear over time.

> 어떤 사람들은 그것을 '소금의 바다'나 '하얀 천국'이라고 부른다. 그것은 세계에서 가장 큰 소금 사막인 Salar de Uyuni이며, 그것은 남아메리카 볼리비아에 위치해 있다.
>
> Salar de Uyuni는 그것의 기이한 풍경으로 유명하다. 이 하얀 사막은 3,650m 높이에 위치해서 태양 아래 밝게 빛난다. 그리고 그곳은 끝이 없어 보인다. <u>사실상 그것은 10,000km²를 넘게 차지한다.</u> 그는 축구 경기장 천오백 개의 크기이다. 이 세상 밖의 어딘가처럼 보이는 것이 당연하다! 게다가 우기 동안에는 훨씬 더 마술 같은 경치가 나타난다. 전체 지역이 거대한 거울이 된다. 땅 위의 얇은 층의 물이 하늘을 선명하게 비춘다. 그것이 사람들로 하여금 그들이 구름 위를 걷고 있는 것처럼 느끼게 한다.
>
> <u>이 놀라운 소금 사막은 어떻게 만들어졌을까?</u> Salar de Uyuni가 항상 소금 사막이었던 것은 아니다. 그것은 큰 해수호의 일부분이었다. 그러나 시간이 흐르면서 볼리비아 산악 지대의 건조한 공기가 모든 물이 사라지게 했다. 이는 백억 톤의 소금을 땅 위에 남겼다. 그 결과 이 놀라운 경치가 만들어졌다!

어휘　heaven[hévən] 몡 천국　desert[dézərt] 몡 사막　locate[lóukeit] 툉 …에 두다[놓다]
unearthly[ʌnə́ːrθli] 혱 기이한　landscape[léndskèip] 몡 풍경　situate[sítʃuèit] 툉 위치시키다
height[hait] 몡 높이　shine[ʃain] 툉 빛나다, 반짝이다　endless[éndlis] 혱 끝없는
scenery[síːnəri] 몡 경치　appear[əpíər] 툉 나타나다 (disappear 툉 사라지다)
giant[dʒáiənt] 혱 거대한　thin[θin] 혱 얇은　layer[léiər] 몡 막, 층　reflect[riflékt] 툉 비추다
highland[háilənd] 몡 산악 지대　billion[bíljən] 몡 10억　[문제] death[deθ] 몡 죽음
take up (시간·공간을) 차지하다　amazed[əméizd] 혱 놀란　confused[kənfjúːzd] 혱 혼란스러운
disappointed[dìsəpɔ́intid] 혱 실망한

구문　7행　**No wonder** it looks like somewhere out of this world!
　　　　・no wonder …: …하는 것이 당연하다
　　　10행　It **makes** people **feel** like they're walking on the clouds.
　　　　・사역동사(make) + 목적어 + 동사원형: …가 ~하게 하다
　　　13행　It **used to be** part of a large saltwater lake.
　　　　・used to-v: '…이었다'라는 의미로, 과거의 지속된 상태를 나타냄
　　　13행　However, the dry air of the Bolivian highlands **caused** all of the water **to disappear** over time.
　　　　・cause + 목적어 + to-v: …가 ~하게 하다

STRATEGIC SUMMARY　desert, rainy, mirror, lake

VOCABULARY REVIEW

A　**1** height　**2** scenery　**3** left　**4** located
B　**1** a　**2** b　　　C　**1** b　**2** a　**3** c　**4** d

unit
06 LITERATURE
pp. 29-32

VOCABULARY PREVIEW

A　**1** b　**2** c　**3** d　**4** a　　　B　**1** damage　**2** guess　**3** return　**4** happen

★A Sherlock Holmes Story

1 b **2** a **3** d **4** it will damage the reputation of the college **5** c **6** a

셜록 홈스는 훌륭한 탐정이다. 어느 날, St. Luke 대학의 교수인 Hilton Soames가 그를 찾아온다. Soams 교수는 도움을 청하며 무슨 일이 일어났는지 설명한다.

내일은 누가 대학 장학금을 받을지 결정하는 시험이 있습니다. 그래서 오늘 오후에 저는 시험지 한 부를 살펴보았습니다. 4시 반에, 저는 친구와의 약속 때문에 시험지들을 제 책상 위에 두고 교수실을 나왔습니다. 한 시간 후에 제가 돌아왔을 때, 저는 문에 열쇠가 꽂혀있는 것을 보았습니다. 저의 하인이 실수로 거기에 두고 간 것이었죠.

저는 교수실에 들어갔고 <u>시험지가 제가 놓아두었던 곳에 있지 않은 것</u>을 알아차렸습니다. 한 장은 바닥에 있었고 다른 한 장은 탁자 위에 있었습니다. 게다가, 저는 제 탁자에서 긁힌 자국을 발견했습니다. 저는 또한 시험지 옆에서 부러진 연필심을 발견했습니다. 그래서 저는 누군가가 급하게 그것들을 베꼈다고 생각합니다. 저는 당신이 내일 시험을 볼 세 학생들을 심문할 필요가 있다고 생각합니다. 그들은 Giles Gilchrist, Daulat Ras, 그리고 Miles McLaren입니다. 그들은 저의 교수실이 있는 동일한 건물에 삽니다.

만일 사람들이 이 사건에 대해 알게 된다면, 대학의 평판에 해를 끼치게 될 것입니다. 홈스 씨, 제발 제가 이 문제를 빠르고 은밀하게 해결할 수 있도록 도와주십시오.

어휘 excellent[éksələnt] 형 훌륭한 detective[ditéktiv] 명 탐정 professor[prəfésər] 명 교수 college[kálidʒ] 명 대학 happen[hǽpən] 동 (일·사건 등이) 일어나다 scholarship[skálərʃip] 명 장학금 copy[kápi] 명 복사본; *(책·신문 등의) 한 부 동 베끼다, 복사하다 appointment[əpɔ́intmənt] 명 약속 return[ritə́:rn] 동 돌아오다 servant[sə́:rvənt] 명 하인 by mistake 실수로 notice[nóutis] 동 알아차리다 scratch[skrætʃ] 명 긁힌 자국 guess[ges] 동 추측하다 in a hurry 급히 question[kwéstʃən] 동 질문하다, 심문하다 incident[ínsədənt] 명 일, 사건 damage[dǽmidʒ] 동 피해를 입히다 reputation[rèpjutéiʃən] 명 평판, 명성 in secret 비밀리에 [문제] case[keis] 명 경우; *사건 mysterious[mistíəriəs] 형 불가사의한, 비밀스러운 note[nout] 명 메모 suspect[səspékt] 동 의심하다

구문 4행 Tomorrow, there is an exam **to decide** [*who* will receive a scholarship to the college].
- to decide: an exam을 수식하는 형용사적 용법의 to부정사
- who 이하는 '의문사(주어) + 동사' 어순의 간접의문문으로, 동사 decide의 목적어 역할을 함

9행 I entered the office and noticed that the papers were not **where** I *had left* them.
- where: '…하는 곳에'라는 의미로, 부사절을 이끄는 접속사
- had left: 주절의 시제보다 앞선 시점의 내용을 가리키는 과거완료

14행 I think you need to question the three students [**who** will take the exam tomorrow].
- who 이하는 the three students를 수식하는 주격 관계대명사절

16행 They live in the same building [**where** my office is].
- where 이하는 the same building을 수식하는 관계부사절

19행 Please, Mr. Holmes, **help** me **solve** this problem quickly and in secret.
- help + 목적어 + 동사원형: …가 ~하도록 돕다

STRATEGIC ORGANIZER copied, original, broken, building

VOCABULARY REVIEW

A **1** secret **2** broken **3** servant **4** copy
B **1** a **2** c   **C** **1** c **2** b **3** d **4** d

8

★unit★
07 SPORTS

pp. 33-36

VOCABULARY PREVIEW

A **1** c **2** a **3** b **4** d   **B** **1** victory **2** automatic **3** divide **4** key

★Ball Possession in Soccer

1 a **2** d **3** b **4** b **5** one team gives the opposing team less time to score **6** 1) F 2) F

축구 경기 중에 텔레비전에 나오는 백분율에 대해 궁금해한 적이 있는가? 그것은 '공 점유율'을 나타낸다. 이것은 한 팀이 공을 가지고 있는 시간의 양이다.

그것은 어떻게 측정되는 것일까? 그것은 자동 분석 장치로 측정된다. 경기장 높이 설치된 16대의 카메라가 경기장의 서로 다른 부분을 녹화하고, 녹화한 것을 컴퓨터로 보낸다. 컴퓨터는 공과 선수들을 점으로 보고, 그들의 움직임을 분석한다. 그러고 나서 그것은 각각의 팀이 얼마나 오랫동안 공을 가지고 있는지 계산한다. 그리고 그것은 한 팀의 시간을 공이 점유된 전체 시간으로 나눈다. 그러나 그 장치는 완벽하지 않다. 그것은 두 선수가 공을 두고 겨룰 때처럼 때때로 실수를 하기도 한다. 그래서 그것은 인간의 도움이 필요하다. 두 명의 사람들이 또한 그 경기를 보고 그 장치가 놓치는 정보를 추가한다.

그런데 우리는 왜 공 점유율에 신경을 쓰는가? 공 점유율이 승리를 보장하지는 않지만, 그것은 우리가 어느 팀이 더 승리할 것 같은지 알 수 있도록 도와준다. 보통, 공을 더 많이 점유한다는 것은 한 팀이 상대 팀에 득점할 시간을 덜 준다는 것을 의미한다. 이것은 종종 경기에서 우승하는 데 있어 중요한 역할을 한다. 그러므로 축구 경기를 볼 때 경기를 더 흥미진진하게 하기 위해 공 점유율에 주목하라!

어휘 wonder[wʌ́ndər] 图 궁금해하다　refer to …을 나타내다　possession[pəzéʃən] 図 소유; *(공을) 차지한 상태 (possess 图 소유하다, 점유하다)　amount[əmáunt] 図 양　automatic[ɔ̀ːtəmǽtik] 図 자동의　analysis[ənǽləsis] 図 분석 (analyze 图 분석하다)　device[diváis] 図 장치　place[pleis] 图 설치하다, 놓다　record[rikɔ́ːrd] 图 녹화하다, 기록하다 (recording 図 녹음, 녹화 (된 것))　field[fiːld] 図 경기장　dot[dat] 図 점　count[kaunt] 图 계산하다　divide[diváid] 图 분할하다; *(…을) …으로 나누다　support[səpɔ́ːrt] 図 지원, 도움　care about …에 관심을 가지다　guarantee[gæ̀rəntíː] 图 보장하다　victory[víktəri] 図 승리　opposing[əpóuziŋ] 図 (팀·군대 등이) 서로 겨루는　key[kiː] 図 중요한, 핵심적인　[문제] advanced[ædvǽnst] 図 선진의　purpose[pə́ːrpəs] 図 용도, 목적　measure[méʒər] 图 측정하다　monitor[mɑ́nətər] 图 감시하다　assist[əsíst] 图 돕다

구문　1행　**Have** you ever **wondered** about the percentages [*shown* on TV during soccer games]?
　　　　　• Have wondered: '…한 적이 있다'의 의미로, 경험을 나타내는 현재완료
　　　　　• shown 이하는 the percentages를 수식하는 과거분사구

　　　7행　Then, it counts [**how** long each team has the ball].
　　　　　• how 이하는 '의문사 + 주어 + 동사' 어순의 간접의문문으로, 동사 counts의 목적어 역할을 함

　　　10행　Two people also watch the game and add information [**that** the device misses].
　　　　　• that 이하는 information을 수식하는 목적격 관계대명사절

　　　13행　…, it helps us know which team **is** more **likely to win**.
　　　　　• be likely to-v: …할 것 같다

　　　15행　This often **plays a** key **role in** [*winning* the game].
　　　　　• play a role in: …에서 역할을 하다
　　　　　• winning 이하는 전치사 in의 목적어 역할을 하는 동명사구

9

VOCABULARY REVIEW

A   *1* scored   *2* guarantee   *3* care about   *4* recorded
B   *1* d   *2* a   C   *1* a   *2* b   *3* d   *4* b

unit 08 PEOPLE

pp. 37-40

VOCABULARY PREVIEW

A   *1* a   *2* d   *3* c   *4* b   B   *1* talent   *2* shortly   *3* recognize   *4* surgery

★Stevie Wonder

1 c   *2* He overcame the difficulties of blindness with his love for music.   *3* c   *4* b   *5* b   *6* a

스티비 원더는 세계에서 가장 잘 알려진 음악가들 중 한 명이다. 당신은 그가 선글라스를 쓰고 무대 위에서 노래하고 있는 모습을 보았을지도 모른다. 그는 비록 출생 직후부터 눈이 멀었지만, 그는 절대로 이것이 그가 음악가가 되는 것을 막도록 하지 않았다. 그는 실명의 어려움을 음악에 대한 사랑으로 극복했다.

어린 소년이었을 때, 그는 음악에 큰 흥미를 보였고 자연스럽게 그것을 배웠다. 열 살이 되기 전 그는 피아노와 하모니카와 같은 다양한 악기들을 완전히 익혔다. (많은 음악가들은 피아노보다 기타를 연주하는 것을 더 좋아한다.) 곧 Motown 레코드사가 그의 재능을 알아보았고 그를 가수로 만들었다. 그가 단 열세 살이었을 때, 그의 앨범 *Fingertips*는 1위의 히트 음반이 되었다. 그때부터 그는 30곡이 넘는 미국 톱 텐 히트곡을 보유하게 되었으며 25개의 그래미상을 받았다.

스티비가 그저 훌륭한 음악가인 것만은 아니다. 그는 또한 다정한 아버지이기도 하다. 그는 한때 자녀들을 보기 위해 눈 수술을 하려고 하기도 했다. 불행히도 그는 눈 상태가 좋지 않았기 때문에 수술을 받을 수 없었다. 그는 또한 자신의 음악을 통해 아이들에 대한 사랑을 나타내기도 한다. 그의 가장 인기 있는 곡들 중 하나인 'Isn't She Lovely'는 그의 첫째 딸 Aisha에 관한 것이다. 팬들은 그의 음악과 성격 둘 다 때문에 스티비를 사랑한다.

어휘   well-known [wélnóun] ⑧ 유명한   musician [mjuːzíʃən] ⑨ 음악가   stage [steidʒ] ⑨ 무대
blind [blaind] ⑧ 눈이 먼 (blindness ⑨ 실명)   shortly [ʃɔ́ːrtli] ⑨ 곧   birth [bəːrθ] ⑨ 출생
discourage [diskə́ːridʒ] ⑧ 막다, 단념시키다   overcome [òuvərkÁm] ⑧ 극복하다
naturally [nǽtʃərəli] ⑨ 자연스럽게   master [mǽstər] ⑧ …을 완전히 익히다
various [vɛ́əriəs] ⑧ 여러 가지의   instrument [ínstrəmənt] ⑨ 기구; *악기
recognize [rékəgnàiz] ⑧ 알아보다   talent [tǽlənt] ⑨ 재능   hit [hit] ⑨ 타격; *히트 곡[음반]
award [əwɔ́ːrd] ⑨ 상   surgery [sə́ːrdʒəri] ⑨ 수술   unfortunately [ʌnfɔ́ːrtʃənətli] ⑨ 불행하게도
character [kǽriktər] ⑨ 성격, 성질   [문제] inner [ínər] ⑧ 내부의   positive [pázətiv] ⑧ 긍정적인
disability [dìsəbíləti] ⑨ 장애   loving [lÁviŋ] ⑧ 다정한   pain [pein] ⑨ 고통
perform [pərfɔ́ːrm] ⑧ 공연하다

구문   1행   Stevie Wonder is **one of the** world's **best-known musicians**.
　　　　　　• one of the + 최상급 + 복수명사: 가장 …한 ~중의 하나
　　　2행   You **may have** *seen* him *singing* on stage [**wearing** sunglasses].
　　　　　　• may have v-ed: …했을지도 모른다
　　　　　　• 지각동사(see) + 목적어 + v-ing: …가 ~하고 있는 것을 보다
　　　　　　• wearing 이하는 동시동작을 나타내는 분사구문
　　　4행   **Though** he's *been* blind since shortly after birth, he never **let** this ***discourage***

him *from becoming* a musician.
- though: '…이긴 하지만'이라는 의미의 접속사
- has been: '(지금까지) …해 왔다'의 의미로, 계속을 나타내는 현재완료
- 사역동사(let) + 목적어 + 동사원형: …가 ～하게 하다
- discourage + 목적어 + from v-ing: …가 ～하는 것을 막다

16행 Once, he tried to have eye surgery **to see** his children.
- to see: '…하기 위해'라는 의미로, 목적을 나타내는 부사적 용법의 to부정사

STRATEGIC ORGANIZER blindness, popular, surgery, love

VOCABULARY REVIEW

A *1* stage *2* musician *3* hit *4* award
B *1* d *2* b   C *1* b *2* c *3* d *4* c

FOOD

pp. 41-44

VOCABULARY PREVIEW

A *1* b *2* d *3* c *4* a   B *1* rich *2* harmful *3* prevent *4* produce

★*Tomatoes*

1 d *2* b *3* Because there were rumors that poisonous substances in tomatoes would turn the blood into acid. *4* b *5* c *6* c

> 매해, 약 1억 2천만 톤의 토마토가 전 세계적으로 생산된다. 전 세계 사람들은 토마토 먹는 것을 즐긴다! 하지만, 19세기에 토마토가 미국에 들어왔을 때, 사람들은 그것들을 먹는 것에 대해 걱정했다. 많은 사람들은 그것들이 아주 해롭다고 생각했다. 그것은 토마토에 있는 독성 물질이 피를 산성으로 변하게 한다는 소문이 있었기 때문이다.
>
> 그러면 사람들은 어떻게 토마토를 먹기 시작하게 되었을까? 전설에 따르면, Robert Gibbon Johnson이라는 이름의 남자가 토마토가 먹기에 안전하다는 것을 증명했다. 그는 군중 앞에서 한 바구니의 토마토를 먹었다. 사람들은 그가 병들어 죽을 것이라고 예상했지만, 그는 그렇지 않았다. 그래서 사람들은 토마토를 먹기 시작했다!
>
> 과거와는 달리, 오늘날 사람들은 토마토가 건강에 아주 좋기 때문에 그것을 좋아한다. 토마토에는 리코펜이라고 불리는 것이 들어 있다. 그것은 심장병과 고혈압, 그리고 심지어 암을 예방하도록 도움을 준다. 토마토는 또한 풍부한 비타민 E를 함유하고 있는데, 그것은 당신의 피부를 아름답게 유지해준다. (해바라기유와 옥수수유 같은 식물성 기름에도 비타민 E가 풍부하다.) 그래서 토마토는 오늘날 많은 음식에 사용된다. 케첩, 파스타 소스, 주스, 그리고 피자가 여기에 포함된다. 토마토는 놀랍지 않은가?

어휘 produce[prədjúːs] ⑧ 생산하다 worldwide[wɔ́ːrldwáid] ⑨ 전 세계에 bring[briŋ] ⑧ 가져오다, 데려오다 harmful[háːrmfəl] ⑨ 해로운 rumor[rúːmər] ⑨ 소문 poisonous[pɔ́izənəs] ⑨ 독이 있는 substance[sʌ́bstəns] ⑨ 물질 acid[ǽsid] ⑨ 산, 산성 legend[lédʒənd] ⑨ 전설 name[neim] ⑧ 이름을 지어주다 prove[pruːv] ⑧ 증명하다 crowd[kraud] ⑨ 군중 expect[ikspékt] ⑧ 예상[기대]하다 ill[il] ⑨ 아픈, 병든 prevent[privént] ⑧ 막다, 예방하다 disease[dizíːz] ⑨ 질병 blood pressure 혈압 cancer[kǽnsər] ⑨ 암 rich[ritʃ] ⑨ 부유한; *…이 풍부한 include[inklúːd] ⑧ 포함하다 [문제] introduce[ìntrədjúːs] ⑧ 소개하다; *들여오다 misunderstood[mìsʌndərstúd] ⑨ 오해를 받는 confuse[kənfjúːz] ⑧ 혼란시키다 maintain[meintéin] ⑧ 유지하다 stomach[stʌ́mək] ⑨ 위 digest[daidʒést] ⑧ 소화시키다

6행 … there were rumors [**that** poisonous substances … blood into acid].
- that: rumors와 동격인 명사절을 이끄는 접속사

8행 According to legend, a man [**named** Robert Gibbon Johnson] proved [*that* tomatoes are safe **to eat**].
- named 이하는 a man을 수식하는 과거분사구
- that: 동사 proved의 목적어인 명사절을 이끄는 접속사
- to eat: '…하기에'의 의미로, 형용사 safe를 수식하는 부사적 용법의 to부정사

11행 The people **expected** him **to get** ill and (**to**) **die**, but he *didn't* (get ill and die).
- expect + 목적어 + to-v: …가 ~할 것으로 예상하다
- didn't 뒤에 반복되는 부분인 get ill and die가 생략됨

18행 Tomatoes also have a lot of vitamin E, **which** *keeps* your skin *beautiful*.
- which: vitamin E를 보충 설명하는 계속적 용법의 주격 관계대명사(= and it)
- keep + 목적어 + 형용사: …을 ~하게 유지하다

STRATEGIC SUMMARY popular, poisonous, healthy, foods

VOCABULARY REVIEW

A **1** legend **2** skin **3** past **4** includes
B **1** a **2** d   C **1** c **2** a **3** d **4** b

unit 10 ECONOMY

pp. 45-48

VOCABULARY PREVIEW

A **1** c **2** a **3** d **4** b   B **1** friendly **2** trust **3** latest **4** advertise

★*Undercover Marketing*

1 b **2** c **3** c **4** c **5** Because people are more likely to trust what their friends say. **6** 1) T 2) F

한 관광객이 당신에게 사진을 찍어달라고 부탁한다. 당신이 동의하자, 그녀는 당신에게 인기 있는 디지털카메라의 최신 모델을 건넨다. 그리고 나서 그녀는 당신에게 그것이 어떻게 작동하는지 보여주고 자신이 그것을 얼마나 좋아하는지 말한다. 그녀는 정말 관광객일까? 사실 그녀는 언더커버 마케팅을 이용해 카메라를 광고하고 있다.

언더커버 마케팅은 일종의 비밀 마케팅이다. 기업들은 제품을 사용하고 그것에 대해 이야기하도록 배우들이나 친절한 사람들에게 돈을 지불한다. 그들은 쇼핑몰과 같이 소비자들이 시간을 보내는 장소에서 그렇게 한다. 하지만 그들은 절대 그들의 목적을 설명하거나 당신에게 어떤 것을 사라고 강요하지 않는다. 그들의 목표는 사람들이 그 제품들을 사고 싶어지도록 자연스러운 방식으로 그것들에 대해 알게 하는 것이다.

요즘, 이러한 종류의 마케팅이 일반적인 광고보다 종종 더 효과적이다. 그것은 많은 사람들이 광고에서 이야기하는 것을 신뢰하지 않고 그것들에 주목하지 않기 때문이다. 또한, 이 마케팅 전략은 구두 추천을 통해 사람들의 관심을 얻는 것을 가능하게 한다. 제품을 사용해 본 사람들은 후기를 쓰고 그것을 친구들에게 추천한다. 사람들은 친구가 이야기하는 것을 신뢰할 가능성이 더 많기 때문에 이것은 효과가 있다. 언더커버 마케팅이 무엇인지 알기 때문에, 당신은 주변의 많은 예들을 알아보게 될 것이다!

어휘 hand[hænd] ⑧ 건네다   latest[léitist] ⑱ 최신의   work[wəːrk] ⑧ 일하다; *작동되다
advertise[ǽdvərtàiz] ⑧ 광고하다   undercover[ʌ̀ndərkʌ́vər] ⑱ 비밀의, 비밀리에 하는
friendly[fréndli] ⑱ 친절한, 우호적인   consumer[kənsúːmər] ⑲ 소비자
hang out (…에서) 시간을 보내다   force[fɔːrs] ⑧ 강요하다   aim[eim] ⑲ 목표

effective[iféktiv] 혱 효과적인   regular[régjulər] 혱 규칙적인; *일반적인, 보통의
commercial[kəmə́:rʃəl] 몡 광고   trust[trʌst] 동 신뢰하다   review[rivjú:] 몡 논평, 비평
recommend[rèkəménd] 동 추천하다 (recommendation 몡 추천)   recognize[rékəgnàiz]
동 알아보다, 인지하다   [문제] unique[ju:ní:k] 혱 독특한   invent[invént] 동 발명하다
method[méθəd] 몡 방법   word-of-mouth[wə́:rdəvmáuθ] 혱 구전의, 구두의   critical[krítikəl]
혱 비판적인

구문   2행   Then she shows you [**how** it works] and tells you [**how** much she likes it].
        • how 이하는 '의문사 + 주어 + 동사' 어순의 간접의문문으로, 각각 동사 shows와 tells의
          직접목적어 역할을 함

        8행   Their aim is to **let** people **know** about the products in a natural way *so that*
        they'll want to buy them.
        • 사역동사(let) + 목적어 + 동사원형: …가 ~하게 하다
        • so that: …하기 위하여

        12행   That's because many people don't trust **what** commercials say and ….
        • what: '…하는 것'의 의미로, 선행사를 포함한 관계대명사

        13행   Also, this marketing strategy makes **it** possible [**to get** people's attention …].
        • it은 가목적어이고, to get 이하가 진목적어

        15행   People [**who** tried a product] write reviews and recommend it to their friends.
        • who 이하는 People을 수식하는 주격 관계대명사절

STRATEGIC SUMMARY   natural, trust, effective, word of mouth

VOCABULARY REVIEW

A   *1* purpose   *2* consumers   *3* product   *4* commercial
B   *1* a   *2* d   C   *1* b   *2* a   *3* a   *4* d

unit 11 FESTIVALS   pp. 49-52

VOCABULARY PREVIEW

A   *1* b   *2* c   *3* a   *4* d   B   *1* wish   *2* wet   *3* luck   *4* symbolize

Songkran

1 c   *2* a   *3* Because April 13th is New Year's Day in the Thai calendar.   *4* b   *5* a, c   *6* d

전 세계의 사람들은 그들만의 방식으로 새해를 기념한다. 어떤 사람들은 다가오는 해를 위해 소원을 빈다. 다른
사람들은 행운을 위해 특별한 음식을 먹는다. 태국에서는 모든 사람들이 새해에 완전히 물에 젖는다!
    태국 사람들은 4월 중순에 사흘에서 열흘 동안 Songkran 축제로 새해를 기념한다. 그것은 1월이 아닌데,
왜냐하면 4월 13일이 태국력으로 설날이기 때문이다. 보통, Songkran은 모든 것을 다시 깨끗하고 새롭게 하는
시기이다. 그래서 사람들은 이 시기에 자신의 집을 청소하거나 마음을 맑게 하기 위해 사원을 방문한다. 하지만
Songkran의 가장 유명한 부분은 물을 끼얹는 것이다. Songkran 기간에 사람들은 서로에게, 심지어는 낯선
이들에게도 물을 끼얹는다. 그들은 마치 물싸움에서처럼 물총, 호스 그리고 양동이를 이용한다! 그것은 정말
재미있으며, 시원한 물은 태국의 뜨거운 4월 날씨에 아주 상쾌하다.

그러면, 왜 사람들은 물을 끼얹는가? 그것은 모든 악운을 씻어내고 새해를 신선한 새로운 시작으로 맞이함을 상징한다. 전통적으로, 사람들은 자신의 가족이나 친구들에게 정중히 한 사발의 물을 부었다. 하지만 그 후에 점점 더 축제 분위기가 되었고, 사람들은 장난스러운 물싸움을 즐기기 시작했다. 당신이 아직도 Songkran에 대해 궁금하다면, 그것을 위해 태국을 방문해 보는 것이 어떤가?

어휘   celebrate[séləbrèit] ⑧ 기념하다, 축하하다   wish[wiʃ] ⑲ 소원   luck[lʌk] ⑲ 행운; *운
festival[féstəvəl] ⑲ 축제 (festive ⑲ 축제의, 축하하는)   temple[témpl] ⑲ 사원, 절   clear[kliər]
⑧ 치우다; *맑게 하다   throw[θrou] ⑧ 던지다   stranger[stréindʒər] ⑲ 낯선 사람   bucket[bʌ́kit]
⑲ 양동이   refreshing[rifréʃiŋ] ⑲ 신선한, 상쾌하게 하는   symbolize[símbəlàiz] ⑧ 상징하다
wash off 씻어내다   misfortune[misfɔ́ːrtʃən] ⑲ 불운   traditionally[trədíʃənəli] ⑨ 전통적으로
politely[pəláitli] ⑨ 정중히   pour[pɔːr] ⑧ 붓다   bowl[boul] ⑲ 그릇   mood[muːd] ⑲ 분위기
playful[pléifl] ⑲ 장난기 많은   curious[kjúəriəs] ⑲ 궁금한, 호기심이 많은   [문제] respect[rispékt]
⑧ 존중하다, 존경하다   totally[tóutəli] ⑨ 완전히   wet[wet] ⑲ 젖은   last[læst] ⑧ 지속되다
a variety of 다양한

구문   2행   **Some** make .... **Others** eat ....
    • some ... others ~: 어떤 사람들은 … 다른 사람들은 ~
    10행   Usually, Songkran is a time for [*making* everything *clean* and *new* again].
    • making 이하는 전치사 for의 목적어로 쓰인 동명사구
    • make + 목적어 + 형용사: …을 ~하게 하다
    12행   ... visit a temple **to clear** their minds at this time.
    • to clear: '…하기 위해'라는 의미로, 목적을 나타내는 부사적 용법의 to부정사
    21행   ..., **how about visiting** Thailand for it?
    • how about v-ing …?: …하는 게 어때?

STRATEGIC SUMMARY   celebrate, clean, throwing, poured

VOCABULARY REVIEW

A   ***1*** wash off   ***2*** stranger   ***3*** misfortune   ***4*** bucket
B   ***1*** a   ***2*** b   C   ***1*** c   ***2*** a   ***3*** c   ***4*** b

unit 12 PSYCHOLOGY   pp. 53-56

VOCABULARY PREVIEW

A   ***1*** b ***2*** c ***3*** a ***4*** d   B   ***1*** bottom ***2*** hungry ***3*** add ***4*** secretly

★*Why People Overeat*

1 d ***2*** c ***3*** d ***4*** c ***5*** Because they eat only until their stomach is full. ***6*** *1)* T *2)* F

무엇 때문에 당신이 과식하게 될까? 당신은 아마 정말 배가 고플 때에만 과식을 한다고 생각할지 모른다. 그러나 이것이 항상 사실인 것은 아니다. 연구는 시각적 신호가 배고픔보다 과식에 더 큰 영향을 준다는 것을 보여준다. 다시 말해서, 당신이 보는 것이 당신이 얼마나 먹는지를 결정할 수 있다.

어휘 cause[kɔːz] 통 야기하다, 초래하다   overeat[òuvəríːt] 통 과식하다   hungry[hʌ́ŋgri] 형 배고픈
(hunger 명 배고픔)   research[risə́ːrtʃ] 명 연구, 조사   visual[víʒuəl] 형 시각의 (vision 명 시력, 시각)
sign[sain] 명 신호, 표시   have an effect on …에 영향을 미치다   determine[ditə́ːrmin]
통 결심하다; *결정하다   bowl[boul] 명 그릇   hidden[hídn] 형 숨겨진   tube[tjuːb] 명 관
bottom[bátəm] 명 바닥, 맨 아래   decrease[diːkríːs] 통 줄다, 감소하다   stomach[stʌ́mək] 명 위
affect[əfékt] 통 영향을 미치다   [문제] be on a diet 다이어트 중이다   secretly[síːkrətli] 부 몰래
add[æd] 통 더하다

구문 1행 What **causes** you **to overeat**?
          • cause + 목적어 + to-v: …가 ~하게 하다
      2행 But this is**n't always** true.
          • not always: '항상 …한 것은 아니다'라는 의미의 부분부정
      4행 In other words, **what** you see can determine [*how* much you eat].
          • what: '…하는 것'의 의미로, 선행사를 포함하는 관계대명사
          • how 이하는 '의문사 + 주어 + 동사' 어순의 간접의문문으로, 동사 determine의 목적어 역할을 함
      6행 In a test, two groups of people **were asked to eat** soup until they felt full.
          • be asked to-v: '…하도록 요구되다'라는 의미의 수동태
      8행 People in group B ate soup from a special bowl [**that** had a hidden tube at the
          bottom].
          • that 이하는 a special bowl을 수식하는 주격 관계대명사절

STRATEGIC SUMMARY overeat, regular, added, disappear

VOCABULARY REVIEW

A **1** tube **2** hunger **3** stomach **4** growing up
B **1** b **2** c   C **1** b **2** d **3** c **4** b

unit 13 SCIENCE
pp. 57-60

VOCABULARY PREVIEW

A **1** d **2** c **3** b **4** a   B **1** impossible **2** send **3** modern **4** improve

Satellites

1 c **2** to learn about the earth's atmosphere **3** b **4** d **5** c **6** d

지금 이 순간, 당신의 머리 위로 날아다니는 수천 개의 물체들이 있다. 그것들은 새나 비행기가 아니다. 더 높은 쪽을 생각해보라. 그것들은 우주로 보내져서 지구 주위를 원을 그리며 이동하는 인공위성들이다!

　　최초의 인공위성은 Sputnik 1호였는데, 그것은 1957년에 소련에서 발사했다. 그것은 공과 같은 모양으로 만들어졌으며 무게는 겨우 83.6kg이었다. 그것의 용도는 지구의 대기를 연구하는 것이었다. 이것 이후로 인공위성 기술은 굉장히 발전되었다. 그러나 수년간 그것은 군대에서만 소유했다.

　　그러나 최근 인공위성 기술은 모든 사람이 사용할 수 있도록 만들어지고 있다. 예를 들어, 인공위성은 오늘날 많은 사람들이 운전하는 것을 도와준다. 당신의 차에 있는 GPS 장치와 함께 작동하는 특별한 무리의 인공위성들이 있다. 이 인공위성들은 당신이 운전할 때 당신의 위치를 추적해서 당신에게 방향 지시를 보내준다. <u>인공위성은 또한 우리에게 내일 날씨가 어떨지도 알려준다.</u> 이는 특별한 카메라가 달린 인공위성이 지구 상의 날씨 변화를 관찰하고 예측하는 데 사용되기 때문에 가능하다. 그리고 위성 텔레비전도 당연히 인공위성을 이용한다. 텔레비전 방송국이 그들의 인공위성에 신호를 보낸다. 이 신호들은 인공위성에 반사해 당신의 텔레비전까지 이동한다. 인공위성이 없는 현대 우리의 삶을 상상하는 것은 불가능하다. 그렇지 않은가?

어휘　object[ɑ́bdʒikt] 몡 물체　　satellite[sǽtəlàit] 몡 인공위성　　send[send] 동 보내다
space[speis] 몡 우주　　launch[lɔːntʃ] 동 발사하다　　shape[ʃeip] 동 …의 모양으로 만들다
weigh[wei] 동 무게가 …이다　　atmosphere[ǽtməsfìər] 몡 대기
technology[teknɑ́lədʒi] 몡 (과학) 기술　　improve[imprúːv] 동 개선되다
belong to … 소유이다, …에 속하다　　military[mílitèri] 몡 군대　　track[træk] 동 추적하다
location[loukéiʃən] 몡 위치　　direction[dirékʃən] 몡 방향; *(pl.) 지시, 명령
possible[pɑ́səbl] 혱 가능한 (impossible 혱 불가능한)　　predict[pridíkt] 동 예측하다
signal[sígnəl] 몡 신호　　bounce[bauns] 동 (소리·빛이) 반사하다　　modern[mɑ́dərn] 혱 현대의
[문제] artificial[àːrtəfíʃəl] 혱 인공의　　sector[séktər] 몡 부문, 분야

구문　1행　Right now, there are thousands of objects [**flying** over your head].
　　　　• flying 이하는 thousands of objects를 수식하는 현재분사구
　　　4행　The first satellite was Sputnik I, **which** was launched by the Soviet Union in 1957.
　　　　• which는 Sputnik I을 보충 설명하는 계속적 용법의 주격 관계대명사
　　　8행　..., however, satellite technologies **have been created** for everyone **to use**.
　　　　• have been created: '…되어 왔다'라는 의미의 현재완료 수동태
　　　　• for everyone: to부정사의 의미상 주어
　　　　• to use: '…하기 위해'라는 의미로, 목적을 나타내는 부사적 용법의 to부정사
　　16행　**It** is impossible [**to imagine** our modern lives without satellites], isn't it?
　　　　• It은 가주어이고, to imagine 이하가 진주어

STRATEGIC ORGANIZER　space, atmosphere, driving, weather

VOCABULARY REVIEW

A　**1** weighs　**2** bounced　**3** location　**4** military
B　**1** c　**2** a　　　C　**1** c　**2** d　**3** c　**4** a

·unit· 14 SOCIETY
pp. 61-64

VOCABULARY PREVIEW

A　**1** a　**2** c　**3** b　**4** d　　　B　**1** offer　**2** set up　**3** employee　**4** normally

★*Pro Bono*

1 c ***2*** It means "for the public good." ***3*** b ***4*** b ***5*** c ***6*** *1)* T *2)* F

> 만약 당신이 특별한 재능이나 기술을 가지고 있다면, 당신은 그것을 다른 사람들을 돕는 데 사용할 수 있다! 이것은 '프로보노' 운동이라고 불린다. 라틴어 용어인 '프로보노'는 '공공의 이익을 위한'이라는 뜻이다. 프로보노 근로자들은 자신의 직장에서 보통 하는 것과 같은 일을 한다. 그러나 차이점은 그들이 어떤 것도 청구하지 않는다는 것이다.
>
> 프로보노 운동의 아이디어는 1970년대에 법조계에서 시작되었다. 많은 가난한 사람들이 변호사 비용을 지불할 수 없어서 법적인 도움을 받지 못했다. 그래서 몇몇 변호사들이 가난한 사람들에게 무료 서비스를 제공하기 시작했다. 곧 많은 사람들이 프로보노 운동이 사회에 도움이 된다는 것을 깨달았다. 후에 의사와 건축업자 같은 다른 전문직 종사자들 또한 프로보노 운동을 하기 시작했다.
>
> 요즘에는 프로보노 운동이 개인에 의해서만 행해지고 있지는 않다. 많은 대기업들은 직원들이 다른 사람들을 도울 기회를 갖도록 프로보노 운동을 조직한다. 예를 들어, 어떤 정보 기술 회사들은 직원들을 학교로 보낸다. 그곳에서 그들은 학생들을 위해 컴퓨터를 설치하는 것을 돕는다. 대기업들이 참여하기 시작한 이후로 프로보노 운동은 점점 더 인기를 끌고 있다. 그래서 이제는 더 많은 사람들이 이것을 하고 있으며, 이는 우리 사회를 개선하고 있다!

어휘   talent[tǽlənt] 몡 재능   skill[skil] 몡 기량; *기술   term[təːrm] 몡 용어   public[pʌ́blik] 혱 공공의 good[gud] 몡 선(善); *이익   normally[nɔ́ːrməli] 튀 보통   charge[tʃaːrdʒ] 통 (요금·값을) 청구하다 legal[líːɡəl] 혱 법률과 관련된   lawyer[lɔ́ːjər] 몡 변호사   realize[ríːəlàiz] 통 깨닫다 professional[prəféʃənl] 몡 전문직 종사자 혱 전문적인   organize[ɔ́ːrɡənàiz] 통 조직하다 employee[implɔ́iiː] 몡 고용인   set up 설치하다   involve[inválv] 통 수반하다; *참여시키다 [문제] joy[dʒɔi] 몡 즐거움   volunteer work 자원봉사   offer[ɔ́ːfər] 통 제공하다   spread[spred] 몡 확산, 전파   for free 무료로

구문   5행   Pro bono workers do the same services [**that** they normally do at their jobs].
- that 이하는 the same services를 수식하는 목적격 관계대명사절

14행   Many big companies organize pro bono work **so that** their employees have chances *to help* others.
- so that: …하기 위하여
- to help: chances를 수식하는 형용사적 용법의 to부정사

17행   **Since** big companies started to get involved, pro bono work *has become* **more and more** popular.
- since: '…이후[부터] (지금까지)'라는 의미로, 주로 현재완료와 함께 쓰임
- has become: '…해 왔다'라는 의미로, 계속을 나타내는 현재완료
- 비교급 + and + 비교급: 점점 더 …한

STRATEGIC ORGANIZER   lawyers, professionals, employees, popular

VOCABULARY REVIEW

A   ***1*** popular   ***2*** realized   ***3*** public   ***4*** lawyer
B   ***1*** b   ***2*** d   **C**   ***1*** b   ***2*** c   ***3*** a   ***4*** d

★*unit* 15 ENTERTAINMENT   pp. 65-68

VOCABULARY PREVIEW

A   ***1*** a   ***2*** d   ***3*** c   ***4*** b   **B**   ***1*** attract   ***2*** award   ***3*** upset   ***4*** move

★Billy Elliot the Musical

1 b **2** c **3** d **4** c **5** Though he was a young boy just like him, his dancing skills were great.
6 d

일기장에게,

오늘 나는 가족과 함께 뮤지컬 빌리 엘리어트를 보러 갔어. 그것은 2005년 런던에서 처음 공연된 이후 전 세계적으로 수백만 명의 사람들을 끌어모았어. 나는 그것이 많은 상을 받았다는 것을 들었고, 그래서 그것을 빨리 보고 싶었어.

뮤지컬 빌리 엘리어트는 같은 제목의 영화에 바탕을 두고 있어. 대본과 노래 가사들은 Lee Hall에 의해 쓰였어. 뮤지컬은 빌리라는 이름의 한 소년에게 초점을 맞추고 있어. 그의 아버지는 그가 권투 선수가 되기를 원하지만 빌리는 자신이 발레 무용수가 되고 싶어 한다는 것을 깨달아. 처음에 그의 아버지는 이 때문에 속상해하시지. 하지만 나중에 그는 빌리를 이해하기 시작하고 그가 꿈을 이룰 수 있도록 도와주셔. 뮤지컬의 모든 것이 굉장했어. 나는 특히 빌리 역할을 한 배우가 좋았어. 그는 나처럼 어린 소년이었지만, 그의 춤 실력은 대단했어!

이 뮤지컬을 보는 동안 나는 춤에 대한 빌리의 열정에 매우 감명을 받았어. 빌리가 "춤을 추고 있을 때 어떤 느낌이 드니?"라는 질문을 받았을 때, 그는 '전기'를 노래하기 시작해. "전기, 전기처럼. 내 안의 불꽃. 그리고 나는 자유로워. 나는 자유로워." 이 가사를 들을 때, 나는 그가 춤을 출 때 얼마나 행복한지 느낄 수 있었어.

어휘 musical[mjúːzikəl] 몡 뮤지컬 attract[ətrǽkt] 동 끌어모으다 million[míljən] 몡 100만
award[əwɔ́ːrd] 몡 상 be based on …에 바탕을 두다 screenplay[skríːnplèi] 몡 영화 대본
lyric[lírik] 몡 (pl.) 가사 boxer[báksər] 몡 권투 선수 realize[ríːəlàiz] 동 깨닫다
achieve[ətʃíːv] 동 성취하다 awesome[ɔ́ːsəm] 혱 굉장한, 엄청난 move[muːv] 동 움직이다;
*감동시키다 passion[pǽʃən] 몡 열정 electricity[ilektrísəti] 몡 전기 spark[spaːrk] 몡 불꽃
[문제] cinema[sínəmə] 몡 영화관 illegally[ilíːgəli] 뷔 불법적으로 running time 상영 시간
upset[ʌ̀psét] 혱 속상한 childhood[tʃáildhùd] 몡 어린 시절

구문 4행 I heard it **had won** many awards, so I *couldn't wait to see* it.
· had won: 주절의 시제보다 앞선 시점의 내용을 가리키는 과거완료
· can't wait to-v: 빨리 …하고 싶어 하다

6행 The musical focuses on a boy [**named** Billy].
· named 이하는 a boy를 수식하는 과거분사구

10행 I especially liked the actor [**who** played Billy].
· who 이하는 the actor를 수식하는 주격 관계대명사절

15행 …, I could feel [**how** happy he was] when he danced.
· how 이하는 '의문사 + 주어 + 동사' 어순의 간접의문문으로, 동사 feel의 목적어 역할을 함

STRATEGIC SUMMARY movie, ballet, dream, passion

VOCABULARY REVIEW

A **1** achieved **2** focus **3** sparks **4** title
B **1** b **2** d   C **1** a **2** d **3** a **4** d

★unit 16 HUMAN BODY pp. 69-72

VOCABULARY PREVIEW

A **1** c **2** d **3** b **4** a   B **1** tough **2** depressed **3** exercise **4** occur

★Runner's High

1 c **2** They feel great both physically and mentally. **3** c **4** b **5** c **6** 1) T 2) F

> 달리기는 힘든 운동이다. 그러므로 당신은 오랜 시간 달리는 것이 더 힘들고 더 고통스러울 것이라고 생각할지도 모른다. 하지만 주자들은 오랜 시간 달릴 때 사실상 덜 피곤하고 심지어 행복하게 느낀다고 말한다. 그는 그들의 몸이 우리를 기분 좋게 만드는 호르몬인 엔도르핀을 만들어내기 때문이다. 이러한 호르몬들이 활성화되는 동안, 주자들은 육체적으로나 정신적으로 모두 기분이 좋아진다. 이러한 경험은 'runner's high'라고 불린다!
>
> runner's high를 느끼려면, 사람들은 30분보다 더 오래 달려야 한다. 그리고 그들은 긴장을 풀고 편안해야 한다. 그래서 힘든 경주를 뛰는 사람들은 보통 그것을 경험하지 않는다. 하지만, runner's high는 달리는 동안에만 발생하는 것은 아니다. 스키 선수, 수영 선수, 테니스 선수와 다른 운동선수들도 이러한 기분을 경험할 수 있다. runner's high가 시작되면, 그들은 아주 좋은 기분을 느끼고 영원히 계속해서 운동하거나 경기를 할 수 있다고 믿는다.
>
> 하지만, 당신은 이러한 기분에 중독되지 않도록 주의해야 한다. runner's high는 빨리 찾아왔다가 사라진다. 그래서 어떤 사람들은 그것을 더 자주 느끼기 위해 너무 많이 운동한다. 이는 그들을 건강하게 하기는커녕 오히려 그들의 근육을 다치게 할 수 있다. 또한 그것은 그들이 운동할 수 없을 때 우울함을 느끼게 할 수 있다. 그러니 이를 기억해라. 지나침은 모자람만큼 해롭다.

어휘　exercise[éksərsàiz] 몡 운동 동 운동하다　painful[péinfəl] 혱 고통스러운　create[kriéit] 동 창조하다, 만들어내다　active[æktiv] 혱 활동적인; *활성의　physically[fízikəli] 뷔 육체적으로　mentally[méntəli] 뷔 정신적으로　experience[ikspíəriəns] 몡 경험 동 경험하다　relaxed[rilǽkst] 혱 느긋한, 편안한　tough[tʌf] 혱 힘든　athlete[ǽθliːt] 몡 운동선수　injure[índʒər] 동 부상을 입히다　muscle[mʌ́sl] 몡 근육　depressed[diprést] 혱 우울한　[문제] regular[régjulər] 혱 규칙적인　reward[riwɔ́ːrd] 몡 보상　occur[əkɔ́ːr] 동 일어나다　addicted[ədíktid] 혱 중독된

구문　7행　That's because their bodies create **endorphins**, **the hormones** [*that* **make** us **feel** good].
- endorphins와 the hormones는 동격
- that 이하는 the hormones를 수식하는 주격 관계대명사절
- 사역동사(make) + 목적어 + 동사원형: …가 ~하게 하다

　　　10행　**While** these hormones are active, runners feel great *both* physically *and* mentally.
- while: '…하는 동안에'라는 의미의 접속사
- both A and B: A와 B 둘 다

　　　18행　…, they feel wonderful and believe they can **keep exercising** or **playing** forever.
- keep v-ing: 계속해서 …하다

　　　22행　**Far from** *making* them *healthy*, this can injure their muscles.
- far from v-ing: 전혀 …이 아닌, …이 아니라 오히려
- make + 목적어 + 형용사: …을 ~하게 하다

STRATEGIC SUMMARY　happiness, hormones, experience, addictive

VOCABULARY REVIEW

A　**1** painful　**2** comfortable　**3** runners　**4** mentally
B　**1** a　**2** a　　**C**　**1** d　**2** d　**3** b　**4** c

VOCABULARY PREVIEW

A   **1** d   **2** a   **3** b   **4** c   B   **1** beginning   **2** remember   **3** smart   **4** randomly

★The Pygmalion Effect

1 b   **2** d   **3** c   **4** d   **5** Because the teacher expected them to do better.   **6** b

> 당신이 교사라고 상상해보자. 만약 당신이 학생들에게 그들이 똑똑하지 않다고 말한다면, 그들은 아마 학급 성적이 나쁠 것이다. 하지만 당신이 그들에게 천재라고 말해준다면, 그들은 아마 잘 해낼 것이다. (수업 중에 필기를 하는 것은 학생들이 수업 내용을 더 잘 기억하도록 도와준다.) 이 상황은 이른바 피그말리온 효과를 설명한다. 피그말리온 효과는 높은 기대를 받는 사람들이 잘 해내고, 낮은 기대를 받는 사람들은 잘 못해낸다고 한다.
>
> 이 효과는 1966년에 캘리포니아의 한 초등학교에서 있었던 실험에서 나타났다. 실험 초반에 연구원들은 한 반에서 몇몇 학생들을 무작위로 선정했다. 그들은 교사에게 이 학생들이 그들의 같은 반 친구들보다 더 똑똑하다고 말해주었다. 놀랍게도, 실험 종료 시에 그들은 무작위로 선정되었던 학생들이 실제로 더 높은 성적을 받았다는 것을 알게 되었다.
>
> 왜 이런 일이 벌어졌을까? 교사는 그들이 더 잘 것이라고 기대했다. 그는 그 학생들에게 관심을 더 쏟았다. 그는 그들을 많이 칭찬했고, 그들의 숙제를 더 주의 깊게 확인하였으며, 그들로부터 좋은 성과를 요구했다. 이 때문에 그 학생들은 더 잘하기 시작했다. 이것은 기대가 얼마나 중요한지를 보여준다. 그러므로 만약 당신이 누군가가 더 잘하길 원한다면, 그저 그들에게서 좋은 것을 기대하라!

어휘   imagine[imǽdʒin] 통 상상하다   smart[smɑːrt] 형 똑똑한   badly[bǽdli] 부 나쁘게
genius[dʒíːnjəs] 명 천재   remember[rimémbər] 통 기억하다   lesson[lésn] 명 수업; *가르침(의 내용)   situation[sìtʃuéiʃən] 명 상황   what is called 소위, 이른바   perform[pərfɔ́ːrm] 통 수행하다   poorly[púərli] 부 좋지 못하게   experiment[ikspérəmənt] 명 실험   beginning[bigíniŋ] 명 시작, 초반   researcher[risə́ːrtʃər] 명 연구원   randomly[rǽndəmli] 부 무작위로   select[silékt] 통 선발하다   surprisingly[sərpráiziŋli] 부 놀랍게도   expect[ikspékt] 통 기대하다 (expectation 명 기대)   extra[ékstrə] 형 추가의   attention[əténʃən] 명 관심, 주의   praise[preiz] 통 칭찬하다   demand[dimǽnd] 통 요구하다   [문제] strict[strikt] 형 엄격한   intelligence[intélədʒəns] 명 지능   relationship[riléiʃənʃip] 명 관계

구문   5행   The Pygmalion effect says that people [**given** high expectations] perform well, and people [**given** low expectations] perform poorly.
   • given 이하는 각각 바로 앞의 people을 수식하는 과거분사구
   16행   The teacher **expected** them **to do** better.
   • expect + 목적어 + to-v: …가 ~하기를 기대하다
   21행   Because of this, the students **started doing** better.
   • doing은 동사 started의 목적어로 쓰인 동명사로, 동사 start는 동명사와 to부정사 모두를 목적어로 취할 수 있음

STRATEGIC ORGANIZER   randomly, smarter, attention, Expecting

VOCABULARY REVIEW

A   **1** genius   **2** effect   **3** badly   **4** praised
B   **1** c   **2** b   C   **1** a   **2** b   **3** c   **4** d

unit 18 TRAVEL

pp. 77-80

VOCABULARY PREVIEW

A *1* a *2* c *3* b *4* d   **B** *1* view *2* fear *3* visitor *4* stunning

Asahiyama Zoo

1 d *2* d *3* b *4* b *5* A special event called the Penguin Walk is held. *6* 1) T 2) F

어제 나는 홋카이도에 있는 Asahiyama 동물원을 방문했다. 전시관은 솜씨 좋게 설계되어 있었다. 방문객들은 동물들의 행동과 그들의 생김새를 아주 가까이에서 관찰할 수 있다. 나는 그곳이 정말 좋았다!

내가 가장 마음에 들었던 곳은 펭귄 수족관이었다. 그곳에는 사방이 유리 벽으로 되어 있는 수중 터널이 있다. 그것은 굉장히 멋진 광경을 선사한다. 터널 안에서, 나는 펭귄이 내 머리 위로 빠르게 수영하는 것을 볼 수 있었다. 나는 그들이 날고 있는 것처럼 느꼈다!

북극곰과 바다표범을 보는 것도 굉장했다. 북극곰들은 물속으로 뛰어들 때 크게 물을 튀겼다. 그리고 바다표범 수족관에는 특별한 유리관들이 있다. 바다표범들은 수영하는 동안 그것들을 통과했다. 나는 겨우 몇 센티미터 떨어져서 그들을 보는 것이 즐거웠다.

나는 오랑우탄을 보는 것도 아주 좋았다. 그들에게는 지상 17미터 위에 있는 타고 놀 거대한 줄들이 있다. 그것은 정말 위험해 보였지만, 그들은 줄에 올라 매달렸다. 자연에서, 오랑우탄은 나무에 산다. 그래서 그들은 그런 높이에서도 두려움을 느끼지 않고 쉽게 돌아다닐 수 있다.

겨울에는 펭귄 워크라고 불리는 특별 행사가 있다고 들었다. 나는 그것을 보러 다시 동물원을 방문하고 싶다!

어휘   exhibit[igzíbit] 명 전시품; *전시회[관]   cleverly[klévərli] 부 교묘하게, 솜씨 좋게   design[dizáin] 동 설계하다   visitor[vízitər] 명 방문객, 손님   behavior[bihéivjər] 명 행동   feature[fí:tʃər] 명 특징; *생김새   aquarium[əkwɛ́əriəm] 명 수족관   underwater[ʌ̀ndərwɔ́:tər] 형 수중의   stunning[stʌ́niŋ] 형 아주 멋진   view[vju:] 명 견해; *광경   polar bear 북극곰   seal[si:l] 명 바다표범   huge[hju:dʒ] 형 거대한   splash[splæʃ] 명 첨벙하는 소리; *(물을) 튀김   pass[pæs] 동 지나가다, 통과하다   giant[dʒáiənt] 형 거대한   rope[roup] 명 끈, 줄   hang[hæŋ] 동 매달리다   height[hait] 명 높이   fear[fiər] 명 두려움   [문제] tourist attraction 관광 명소   scenery[sí:nəri] 명 경치, 풍경   tube[tju:b] 명 관, 통

구문   6행   Inside the tunnel, I could **see** penguins **swimming** fast above my head.
• 지각동사(see) + 목적어 + v-ing: …가 ~하고 있는 것을 보다

7행   I felt **as if they were** flying!
• as if + 가정법 과거: 마치 …인 것처럼

9행   [**Seeing** the polar bears and seals] was great, too.
• Seeing 이하는 문장의 주어 역할을 하는 동명사구

14행   They have a giant set of ropes **to play on** [*that* is 17 meters off the ground].
• to play on: a giant set of ropes를 수식하는 형용사적 용법의 to부정사구
• that 이하는 a giant set of ropes를 수식하는 주격 관계대명사절

STRATEGIC ORGANIZER   tunnel, splash, tubes, skillful

VOCABULARY REVIEW

A *1* huge *2* underwater *3* exhibit *4* rope
B *1* a *2* b   **C** *1* a *2* b *3* c *4* d

unit
19 **FASHION**   pp. 81-84

VOCABULARY PREVIEW

A *1* a *2* c *3* d *4* b   B *1* status *2* copy *3* recent *4* directly

★*The History of Wigs*

1 c *2* a *3* Because the hot desert sun would shine directly onto their bald heads. *4* c *5* c
6 1) F 2) T

> 오늘날 많은 사람들이 가발 착용하는 것을 아주 좋아한다. 그러나 이것은 단지 최근의 패션은 아니다. 가발은 전 역사에 걸쳐 착용되어 왔다. 또한 그것들은 시간과 장소에 따라 다른 역할을 해왔다.
>
> 고대 이집트 시대에는 사람들이 실용적인 이유들로 가발을 썼는데, 자신의 머리를 깨끗하게 유지하고 태양으로부터 머리를 가리기 위해서였다. 그 당시에 그들은 이가 생기는 것을 방지하려고 삭발했다. 하지만 그것은 뜨거운 사막의 태양이 곧장 그들의 대머리 위에 비친다는 것을 의미했다. 그래서 그들은 머리를 보호하기 위해 가발이 필요했다.
>
> 16세기부터 18세기까지 서유럽에서는 가발을 쓰는 것이 자신의 <u>사회적 지위</u>를 나타내는 하나의 방법이었다. 영국의 여왕 엘리자베스 1세와 프랑스의 루이 13세가 외모를 개선하기 위해 가발을 쓰자, 상류 계급들이 그들을 모방하기 시작했다. 곧 가발은 아주 인기가 많아졌다. 그러나 모든 사람들이 가발을 쓰도록 허용되지는 않았다. 왕족과 고위 관료들만 그것을 쓸 수 있었다. (고위 관료들에게는 많은 하인들이 있었다.) 그래서 가발을 쓰는 것은 사회에서 한 사람의 높은 위치를 상징하게 되었다. 이제 가발은 더 이상 이런 목적으로 착용되지는 않는다. 하지만 영국 법정의 판사들은 오랜 전통을 존중하기 위해서 여전히 흰색 가발을 쓴다.

어휘   wig[wig] 명 가발   recent[ríːsnt] 형 최근의   throughout[θruːáut] 전 … 동안, … 내내
practical[præktikəl] 형 실용적인   hide[haid] 동 숨다; *가리다, 감추다   shave[ʃeiv] 동 면도하다
avoid[əvɔ́id] 동 막다, 방지하다   desert[dézərt] 명 사막   directly[diréktli] 부 곧장
bald[bɔːld] 형 대머리의   protect[prətékt] 동 보호하다   upper[ʌ́pər] 형 위쪽의
class[klæs] 명 계급   copy[kápi] 동 복사하다; *모방하다, 따라 하다   royalty[rɔ́iəlti] 명 왕족
high-ranking[háiræŋkiŋ] 형 고위의   official[əfíʃəl] 명 관리   symbol[símbəl] 명 상징
judge[dʒʌdʒ] 명 판사   court[kɔːrt] 명 법정   honor[ánər] 동 존중하다   [문제] industry[índəstri]
명 산업   material[mətíəriəl] 명 재료   status[stéitəs] 명 신분, 지위

구문   2행   Wigs **have been worn** throughout history.
· have been worn: '…되어 왔다'라는 의미의 현재완료 수동태
7행   At that time, they shaved off their hair **to *avoid*** *getting* lice.
· to avoid: '…하기 위해'라는 의미로, 목적을 나타내는 부사적 용법의 to부정사
· avoid는 동명사를 목적어로 취하는 동사
11행   …, wearing wigs was a way **to show** one's social status.
· to show: a way를 수식하는 형용사적 용법의 to부정사
14행   However, **not everyone** was allowed to wear wigs.
· not everyone: '모두가 …인 것은 아니다'라는 의미의 부분부정

STRATEGIC ORGANIZER   shaving, sun, status, upper

VOCABULARY REVIEW

A *1* shave *2* social *3* honor *4* court
B *1* c *2* b   C *1* a *2* c *3* b *4* c

VOCABULARY PREVIEW

A **1** c **2** a **3** b **4** d   B **1** safety **2** stressed **3** pain **4** useful

★Animal Testing

1 b **2** d **3** scientists have invented many kinds of medicine that help animals stay healthy
4 d **5** b **6** b

> 과학자들은 신약의 안전성을 테스트하기 위해서 때때로 동물을 사용한다. 어떤 사람들은 이것이 필요하다고 생각하지만, 다른 사람들은 그것이 금지되어야 한다고 생각한다.
>
> Jason: 저는 사람의 목숨을 구하는 것이 가장 중요한 것이라고 생각합니다. 약은 사람들에게 사용되기 전에 테스트를 받아야 합니다. 오랫동안 동물 실험은 약이 안전한지를 알아보는 최선의 방법이었습니다. 실험에서 동물을 사용하지 않고는 과학자들은 끔찍한 질병에 대한 치료법을 찾을 수 없을 것입니다.
>
> Amy: 동물들도 사람들처럼 고통을 느낄 수 있습니다! 많은 동물들이 실험에서 고통을 받고 죽습니다. 우리에게는 동물들에게 잔인할 권리가 없습니다. 과학자들은 동물들을 해치지 않는 신약 실험법을 찾아야 합니다. 동물의 생명도 사람의 생명만큼이나 중요합니다.
>
> Patrick: 동물 실험은 사람들뿐만 아니라 동물들에게도 유용합니다. 과학자들은 동물들이 건강을 유지하도록 도와주는 여러 종류의 약들을 개발해왔습니다. 하지만 이는 동물 실험 없이는 가능하지 않았을 것입니다.
>
> Sue: 동물 실험이 정말 효과적인가요? 과학자들은 새로운 종류의 약이 쥐에게는 해를 끼치지 않는다는 것을 발견할 수 있습니다. 하지만 그것이 반드시 사람에게도 해가 없으리라는 것을 의미하지는 않습니다. 더욱이, 어떤 보고서들에 따르면 실험동물들은 너무 스트레스를 받아서 결과들이 항상 정확한 것은 아니라고 합니다.

어휘   safety[séifti] 명 안전(성)   medicine[médsn] 명 약   ban[bæn] 동 금지하다
cure[kjuər] 명 치료법   terrible[térəbl] 형 끔찍한, 심한   disease[dizíːz] 명 질병
pain[pein] 명 통증, 고통   suffer[sʌ́fər] 동 고통받다   right[rait] 명 권리   cruel[krúːəl] 형 잔혹한
useful[júːsfəl] 형 유용한   report[ripɔ́ːrt] 명 보고서   stressed[strest] 형 스트레스를 받는
accurate[ǽkjurət] 형 정확한   [문제] method[méθəd] 명 방법

구문   5행   Medicine **must be tested** before it is used on people.
　　　　　• must be tested: '…되어져야 한다'라는 의미로, 조동사와 함께 쓰인 수동태
　　　　6행   ..., animal testing has been the best way to find out [**if** medicine is safe].
　　　　　• if: '…인지 (아닌지)'라는 의미의 접속사로, 동사구 find out의 목적어인 명사절을 이끎
　　　　8행   **Without** using animals in their experiments, scientists **wouldn't be** able to find cures for terrible diseases.
　　　　　• '…가 없다면 ~할 텐데'의 의미의 가정법 과거 문장으로, without이 이끄는 구가 if절을 대신함
　　　　21행   But that does**n't necessarily** mean that it won't harm humans!
　　　　　• not necessarily: '반드시[꼭] …은 아니다'라는 의미의 부분부정
　　　　23행   ..., test animals get **so** stressed **that** the results aren't always accurate.
　　　　　• so … that ~: 너무 …해서 ~하다

STRATEGIC ORGANIZER   *1)* Humans   *2)* pain   *3)* animal   *4)* safe

VOCABULARY REVIEW

A **1** cure **2** right **3** invented **4** report
B **1** a **2** b   C **1** d **2** b **3** a **4** d

MEMO